The Opportunity

Richard N. Haass

The Opportunity

●

*America's Moment
to Alter History's Course*

PublicAffairs
NEW YORK

BOOK DESIGN AND COMPOSITION BY JENNY DOSSIN. TEXT SET IN ADOBE CASLON.

Library of Congress Cataloging-in-Publication Data
Haass, Richard.
The Opportunity : America's moment to alter history's course/Richard N. Haass.
p. cm.
Includes bibliographical references and index.
ISBN-13 978-1-58648-276-3; ISBN 1-58648-276-9
1. United States—Foreign relations—2001- 2. National security—United States. 3. World politics—1989- 4. Security, International. I. Title.
E902.H22 2005
327.73'009'051—dc22
2005045807

FIRST EDITION

PBK: ISBN-13 978-1-58648-453-8; ISBN 1-58648-453-2

10 9 8 7 6 5 4 3 2 1

To Sam and Francesca:
May our opportunity become your future

The Future has many names
For the weak it is unattainable
For the fearful it is unknown
For the bold it is opportunity

·

Victor Hugo

CONTENTS

Preface to
the Paperback Edition

Mᴏʀᴇ ᴛʜᴀɴ ᴏɴᴇ ʀᴇᴀᴅᴇʀ will wonder why a book titled *The Opportunity* is being reissued now. Today's headlines—nascent civil war in Iraq, new terrorist threats, conflict in Lebanon, genocide in Darfur, the failure of world trade talks, mounting concern over nuclear programs in Iran and North Korea, oil at record prices—hardly conjure images of possibility.

As is sometimes the case, though, appearances can be deceiving. Notwithstanding these serious crises, a meaningful opportunity to promote order in the world continues to exist. Having said this, it is important to be precise about the opportunity at hand. It is decidedly different from the sort envisioned by those who favor (unwisely, in my view) an American foreign policy premised on making democracy the norm and who believe that the opportunity to effect a broad democratic transformation exists. It is also fundamentally different from the sort of opportunity believed to be inherent in most every crisis. It is not at all clear that much in the way of opportunity does, in fact, exist on the streets of Baghdad or Beirut. The maxim that "things have to get worse before they get better" does not necessarily hold in a part of the world whose history suggests that things often get worse before they get even worse.

Rather, the notion of opportunity in this book is one that is more structural. It is premised on the judgment that, for the foreseeable future, the risk of great power conflict is minimal. This condition creates the potential for the United States and other leading countries to work together to tackle the regional and global challenges that increasingly define our era. If they do cooperate—and the argument will be made that they have good reason, at times even a moral obligation to—an opportunity exists to create a world that provides basic security, a decent standard of living, and essential freedoms for most of its inhabitants.

This vision is, to be sure, optimistic. But it is not naïve. Distant and recent history alike suggests substantial cooperation among states is possible. It will not just materialize on its own, however. The challenge to the United States and other governments is to translate opportunity into reality. One hopes they are up to the challenge, for this also happens to be an opportunity borne of necessity. Either we bring about meaningful international cooperation or we risk being overwhelmed by destructive forces both old and new.

RICHARD N. HAASS,

August 2006

PREFACE

CHARLES DE GAULLE is said once to have turned to the fashionable woman seated next to him at a dinner party and, trying to make conversation, asked her what she thought of history. She said something to the effect that she loved history. De Gaulle, shocked that anyone could see history in a positive light in the wake of two world wars, coolly replied, "I don't," turned away, and spent the remainder of the evening speaking to the woman seated on his other side.

Every now and then, though, history surprises us and produces something distinctly positive. We are now—meaning not simply today, but the decade and a half since the Berlin Wall came down, thereby ending the Cold War—experiencing one of those times.

What history has given us is a rare, precious, but fragile opportunity to usher in an age of considerable peace, prosperity, and freedom. What motivates this book is a deep concern that the United States is not taking full advantage of the opportunity. During the 1990s, the Clinton administration did too little to shape the world; more recently, the administration of George W. Bush has often tried to do too much or has tried to do too many things in the wrong way. The result, though, is the same: We risk squandering the historic opportunity at hand.

It is roughly a decade since I wrote a book published under the title *The Reluctant Sheriff*. The book argued that the post–Cold War world was relatively unstructured—a modern version of the nineteenth-century American "Wild West"—and that in the absence of standing arrangements for dealing with the challenges of the post–Cold War world, the United States would have to organize and lead coalitions of willing and able states and organizations (posses) to meet the challenges of the day. My concern at the time was that the Clinton administration, with its domestic-first bias— "It's the economy, stupid"—was for the most part opposed to investing the time and resources needed to succeed in the world and that we would waste the extraordinary opportunity before us.[1]

I would not write such a book today. The world is much changed. We are operating not only in the post–Cold War period, but we are also well into the post-9/11, post–Afghan war, and post–Iraq war era. Arguably even more changed is the United States and U.S. foreign policy. The sheriff could hardly be described as reluctant. Admirers of the foreign policy of George W. Bush might settle on "resolute," critics on "reckless." Either way, foreign policy and national security are again American priorities, and the United States is willing (as we have seen) to use its immense power, especially military power, with few followers if and when it so decides.

Despite several recent positive developments, the United States is not always succeeding. Anti-Americanism is at record levels. It is easier to wage and win wars than to consolidate and negotiate peace. Democracy is difficult to instill and impossible to install. Military primacy is not to be confused with security, much less invulnerability. In short, Americans cannot successfully manage the challenges of globalization on their own.

The ideas that inform this book took shape over the past several years. I was director of policy planning in the Department of State from early 2001 through mid-2003, and in that capacity worked closely with Colin Powell, Condoleezza Rice, and others on some of the central foreign policy endeavors of the administration. This included helping to develop the National Security Strategy published in September 2002, a strategy that embraced the importance to the United States of building and maintaining good relations with the other major powers. Several months before the document was published, in April 2002, I delivered a speech to the Foreign Policy Association in which I discussed this theme in greater detail. Many of these ideas were further refined in an address I gave in March 2004 to the National Committee on American Foreign Policy on the occasion of my receiving the Hans J. Morgenthau Award. By then, this book was well under way, but the reaction to what I had to say encouraged me to complete it.

The first draft of *The Opportunity* was completed on November 1, 2004, the day before the presidential election, and was written without knowing who would win. The intent was to produce a book that would be equally relevant to a second Bush or first Kerry administration. I held off publishing this book in the run-up to the November election for another reason, however: I did not want it to be seen in a political light or in any way as an attempt on my part to influence the outcome of the election. I say all this not out of an inflated sense of my own significance, but because the words of a former official can sometimes have an impact that has more to do with politics and timing than with the quality of his or her ideas.

At the time of this writing, I am president of the Council on Foreign Relations, an independent, national membership organization and a center for scholars dedicated to producing and disseminating ideas so that people everywhere can better understand the foreign policy choices facing the United States and other governments. The Council is an organization that is nonpartisan at and to its core. I do not speak for the Council, which takes no institutional positions. Nor do I speak for its many individual or corporate members, who are fiercely independent. This book represents my thinking, no more and (I hope) no less.

RICHARD N. HAASS
New York, NY
March 2005

I

•

The Opportunity
to Define an Era

THE CURRENT WORLD situation seems depressing, at times overwhelming. Terrorism is now a part of the fabric of modern life; at best we live with it, at worst we will die from it. It is a question of "when" and not "if" the United States will suffer from another major act of terrorism, possibly one involving a weapon of mass destruction. North Korea and Iran have made substantial strides in producing nuclear explosive material and, in the case of North Korea, in developing nuclear weapons. Peace in the Middle East between Israelis and Palestinians remains distant. A large proportion of the world's population is mired in poverty, with nearly 3 billion people, close to half the population of the planet, subsisting on $2 a day or less. Their plight is often exacerbated by HIV/AIDS and other infectious diseases. Darfur (in Western Sudan) is but the most recent in a long line of tragedies highlighting the reality that the greatest threat to many individuals around the world stems from the actions of their own governments and their fellow citizens. Protectionism has made a comeback as efforts to extend free trade continue to run up against special interests in Europe, the United States, and elsewhere. And, after impressive battlefield victories, the United States has found it extraordinarily difficult to stabilize either Afghanistan or Iraq. Iraq in particular has proved to be an expensive war of choice, one that has triggered an intense debate in the United States and around the world over American foreign policy and how the United States should use its immense power. Indeed, not since Vietnam, the last costly war of choice fought by the United States, has American foreign policy proved to be as controversial and as unpopular either at home or abroad.

Yet despite these and other difficulties, this continues to be a moment of rare opportunity for the United States and for the world. The United States, working with the governments of the other major powers, can still shape the course of the twenty-first century and bring about a world that is to a striking degree characterized by peace, prosperity, and freedom for most of the globe's countries and peoples.

Opportunity, though, is just that. It represents possibility, not inevitability. This explains in part why we live in a time variously described as the post–Cold War or post-9/11 world. Such descriptions tell us where we have been, not where we are, much less where we are heading. Only when we see what the United States and the world make of this opportunity will the current era earn its name. This could turn out to be an era of prolonged peace and prosperity, made possible by American primacy successfully translated into influence and effective international arrangements. Or it could turn out to be an era of gradual decay, an incipient modern Dark Ages, brought on by a loss of control on the part of the United States and the other major powers and characterized by a proliferation of weapons of mass destruction (WMD), failed states, and growing terrorism and instability.[1] Still a third possibility is that this period will come to be viewed as another interwar era, or more precisely an inter–Cold War era, bracketed by the half-century struggle with the Soviet Union on the one hand and another such competition on the other, most likely between the United States and China.

At the heart of the opportunity is the fact that we live at a time when the prospect of war between states is less common than has been the case for several centuries and in which the prospect of conflict between this era's major powers is remote. President George W. Bush made just this point in his introduction to his administration's 2002 National Security Strategy: "Today, the international community has the best chance since the rise of the nation-state in the seventeenth century to build a world where great powers compete in peace instead of continually prepare for war."[2] It is difficult to exaggerate the significance of this development. It represents a fundamental departure from the past several hundred years of history, throughout which the defining struggle in the world was largely one between and among major powers. The twentieth century, for example, was dominated by a struggle between essentially liberal countries (led by Great Britain, France, and the United

States) and militarized tyrannies (Germany and Japan in the first half of the century, the Soviet Union in the latter). This struggle was punctuated by three world wars, two of which were intensely hot, the third mostly (and mercifully) cold. There were existential threats to the United States and its allies, but these threats emanated from great power rivals.

The twenty-first century is fundamentally different. For the first time in modern history, the major powers of the day—currently, the United States, Europe, China, Russia, Japan, possibly India—are not engaged in a classic struggle for domination at each other's expense. There are few contests over territory. For the foreseeable future, war between or among them borders on the highly unlikely and, in some cases, the unthinkable.

There is no fundamental ideological fault line pitting one great power against another in the world, and certainly nothing comparable to the "Communism versus Free World" axis that defined the previous era. Many governments share the view that "new forces," including terrorism, disease, and the spread of weapons of mass destruction, constitute the greatest threats to security and stability. And all the major powers (as well as virtually all countries, medium and small alike) share a stake in maintaining the stability that provides a necessary context for the economic interactions that benefit everyone.

In addition, the number of countries that can be accurately portrayed as full or near democracies (more than 100) is the highest in history; the same can be said for market economies.[3] All this bodes well, not just for projected levels of human freedom and prosperity, but also for peace, as there is a good deal of scholarship suggesting that mature democracies are less likely to wage war on one another than countries where democracy has not put down deep roots or where it exists not at all.[4]

We do not owe this good fortune to nuclear deterrence, the linchpin of peace between the two dominant powers throughout the Cold War. Although deterrence remains in effect, today's major powers do not worry actively about each other's nuclear intentions. More significant is the fact that U.S. strength—particularly military strength—is so pronounced that it discourages any kind of direct aggression from another state. Just as important, and recent intense disagreements over Iraq and other issues notwithstanding, international acceptance or at least tolerance of American power and purpose remains sufficiently high that other powers are not inclined as a matter of reflex to resist what the United States does around the world. None of the other major powers sees the United States as some contemporary version of, say, late-nineteenth-century Germany, a country intent on continental domination and colonial conquest that, as a result, had to be countered.

In history, no single country has ever possessed greater strength, and few countries or empires have enjoyed such advantages over their contemporaries as the United States does today. The United States now spends on the order of

$500 billion a year on defense, more than China, Russia, India, Japan, and all of Europe combined. The qualitative advantage of the U.S. military is such that no other country can compete with the mobility, accuracy, and lethality of the U.S. forces. There is no obvious counterbalance: Today's world is characterized by dramatic American advantage—a decided *imbalance* of power.

What is more, the United States enjoys the rare luxury of focusing almost all its defense budget abroad—in Europe, Asia, and the broader Middle East. Even allowing for sharply increased spending on homeland security introduced in the wake of 9/11, the United States spends only 10 to 15 percent of its security dollars on what might be described as self-defense against external threats. Historically, major powers have spent a significant portion of their resources fending off powerful, unfriendly neighbors. By contrast, the two immediate neighbors of the United States are its two largest trading partners. There is no significant threat in the Western Hemisphere. Consequently, much of what the United States devotes to national security is available for use elsewhere around the world.

American power is also economic. The GDP of the United States, more than $11 trillion, is more than 20 percent of world output, equal to the total annual output of goods and services of all twenty-five countries of the European Union (EU) combined, or to that of Japan, Germany, the United Kingdom, France, and China. Global economic performance is tightly linked to American economic performance. Access to the American market is essential; the United States, with just under 5 percent of the world's population, imports 18 percent of what the rest of the world exports. American investment is often a principal driver of economic development elsewhere. The dollar remains the closest thing that there is to an international currency.

U.S. political weight is no less significant. When the United Nations was conceived in the 1940s, the United States was one of five permanent members of the Security Council accorded veto power. The United States was first among equals then and remains so today. In situations ranging from the Middle East and North Korea to Colombia and Sudan, the United States is the proverbial 800-pound gorilla, whether it is in the room or not. What the United States chooses to do, what it chooses not to do, can and often does have profound consequences. This political influence is reinforced by American cultural reach: the influence of American universities, Hollywood and American television, U.S.-based media, and ideas generated throughout American society. The United States is both a model and an agent of global change.

All this power does not guarantee an age of perpetual peace or mean that history is ended or that we are secure. It is possible that traditional challenges to American dominance will emerge. One of the challenges for U.S. foreign policy is to ensure that great power competition does not revive on the scale of previous eras. Unfortunately, the first fifteen years of the post–Cold War era do not provide much reason for optimism on this score. Unless there are significant changes to U.S. foreign policy, we will almost certainly see a return to a world defined by balance of power politics, one in which the United States and other major powers will find themselves distracted by one another and unable to devote their resources to taking on what are in fact the real challenges of the day, those stemming from globalization and from a number of medium-sized and weak states.

U.S. strength, as considerable as it is and is likely to remain, is not unlimited. The number of active duty U.S. military personnel is approximately 1.4 million, down from just over 2 million at the end of the Cold War. Although some of this reduction can be attributed to improvements in technology and tactics, which in turn make possible reducing the number of troops without reducing overall combat effectiveness, the fact remains that quality cannot always substitute fully for quantity. Some tasks (in particular those that do not involve combat on open battlefields such as post-conflict stability operations) require a great deal of manpower. The result is that the United States would be hard pressed to respond to a full-fledged crisis on the Korean Peninsula without reducing its commitment to Iraq—or to try to replicate anywhere else what it is doing in Iraq or to intervene on a large scale in some humanitarian crisis such as in Darfur.

The United States is also stretched financially. The U.S. government, which could boast a sizable budget surplus

only a few years ago, now runs a fiscal deficit of more than
$400 billion a year, a result of lower taxes, slower than
hoped for economic growth, and an enormous increase in
spending on both entitlements (mostly retirement and
health-related) and discretionary items, that is, everything
else, from homeland security and defense to education and
roads. It is impossible to avoid questions of how American
society will take care of its own as baby boomers retire and
as life expectancy continues to increase.[5] Making matters
worse is the simultaneous mushrooming of the current account (essentially trade) deficit, which is now more than
$600 billion a year, a figure approaching 6 percent of GDP.
The American economy increasingly depends on the willingness of foreign governments and institutions to hold on
to vast pools of dollars. The current situation may well endure for some time, given that it suits the immediate interests of all parties, but it cannot and will not endure
indefinitely. (To paraphrase the economist Herb Stein,
"[T]hat which cannot go on indefinitely, won't.") It is only
a matter of time before foreigners grow wary (not to mention weary) of continuing to accumulate dollars, and when
they do they will elect to sell some of those dollars they
possess or slow their rate of accumulating additional ones.
As this happens, the only question is whether the adjustment in the dollar's value downward is gradual and man-
ageable or quick and extremely painful in its effects.

To be sure, the United States could adopt policies that
would increase its military capability or reduce its economic

vulnerability. The United States could afford to increase military spending without jeopardizing the American economy. The United States spent a much higher percentage of its GDP on defense during World War II, for instance. But additional large increases in defense spending would increase the scale of the deficit and crowd out federal spending for more popular programs. Similarly, the United States could increase taxes, or decrease discretionary spending or what it spends on entitlements or both, but significant changes are politically unrealistic. A draft would likely be opposed by a majority of the American people, and already there are signs of popular resistance to heavy dependence upon and use of reserve forces.

These considerations all emphasize the unsuitability of American democracy for an imperial role.[6] The American people are prepared to sacrifice for costly wars of necessity, such as World War II, and to undertake wars of choice such as the interventions in both Bosnia and Kosovo, so long as they do not prove to be costly. But expensive wars of choice (such as Vietnam proved to be and as Iraq threatens to become) that call for open-ended sacrifice for uncertain ends are simply not sustainable.

There is also the matter of American vulnerability. Indeed, with the possible exception of ten days in October 1962 when the United States and the Soviet Union nearly came to war over the introduction of Soviet missiles into Cuba, Americans and their country have never felt more insecure.

American vulnerability is real. In part it is the residue of the Cold War and the fact that Russia still possesses thousands of nuclear warheads, more than enough to obliterate the United States. There is also China's small but growing (and improving) nuclear arsenal. More of a danger, though, is the large Russian stockpile of nuclear materials (and possibly biological and chemical agents or weapons) that one day could end up in the hands of states such as North Korea and Iran or groups such as al Qaeda. Or terrorists could locate another source of advanced weapons or even develop their own basic weapon of mass destruction.[7] Even without such a development, and as September 11 so starkly revealed on television screens across the country and the world, today's terrorists can readily enter and move about the United States and cause billions of dollars of damage and claim thousands of lives with nothing more advanced than box cutters. What the United States has spent on homeland security has made airports somewhat safer but not much else.[8]

The domestic vulnerability highlights a military weakness. Dominance on traditional battlefields, where advanced land, air, and sea-based forces can be combined, is one thing; dominance in built-up urban areas is something quite different. Many U.S. military advantages are irrelevant to the challenge of nation- or state-building in places such as Afghanistan and Iraq. A lesson many governments and individuals seem to have taken from the 1991 Gulf War and from the more recent Afghanistan and Iraq wars is that the one place *not* to challenge the United States is on a traditional battlefield using traditional tools of war. Terrorism and weapons of mass destruction are emerging as the preferred "equalizers."

The United States is vulnerable in other ways as well. The United States increasingly depends on imports of oil and natural gas; even more fundamentally, the American and world economies run on fossil fuels. Loss of adequate supply of oil or natural gas or price spikes could cause economic disruptions, trigger inflation, and undermine economic growth. Energy is one expression of economic interdependence. Millions of jobs depend on the ability to export goods and services around the world. Imports provide necessary goods and services, not to mention quality and choice. If trade protectionism were to make a comeback, it would have a chilling effect on the U.S. and global economies. At the same time, the willingness of others to hold billions of dollars allows Americans to import more than they export and to spend more as a government than is taken in. If foreigners were to have second thoughts about their dollar holdings, the need to hike interest rates in order to attract dollars to fund the U.S. debt and attract resources for investment would likely trigger job loss and recession in the United States.

America is also susceptible to global perils. In 2003, the outbreak of SARS in China demonstrated, like HIV/AIDS and the flu before it, that viruses respect no border. When people in China sneezed, people in Canada and the United

States caught much more than a cold. Viruses of another sort, those carried in cyberspace that infect computers, can wreak havoc on a modern society. Worldwide drug trafficking meets and fuels American demand (and is indirectly responsible for a significant portion of our crime). Global climate change is another sort of American vulnerability. It is broadly understood that the way energy is used around the world is altering the temperature of the atmosphere, something that before too many more decades pass could alter the ability to grow crops or live in coastal areas.

Many of these vulnerabilities are manifestations of globalization, which at its core is the increasing volume, speed, and importance of flows within and across borders of people, ideas, greenhouse gases, manufactured goods, dollars, euros, television and radio signals, drugs, germs, e-mails, weapons, and a good deal else. What is at issue is not simply the fact that the actions of one government affect and are affected by those of others, but also the reality that many of the most important forces in the world are beyond the control and, in some cases, even knowledge of governments.

Many aspects of globalization are positive, including the Internet, travel, trade, financing of investment, faxes, and telephones. Many of these phenomena play to U.S. strengths, as Americans (given their relatively open, dynamic society) are well suited to the demands of a modern world economy. Indeed, globalization is a powerful force behind the improvement in the American standard of living and, in some cases, the quality of life the United States provides its citizens.

The coexistence of what might be described as forces of disorder and order in the world at the same time is nothing new. Indeed, history can be understood as the balance or struggle between them. The best book that I have read on international affairs, and the one that most influenced my own thinking—Hedley Bull's *The Anarchical Society*—captures in its title this fundamental truth, namely, that at any moment the world is a blend of restraint and rules (society) and anarchy. History, then, is largely determined by the degree to which the major powers of the era can agree on rules of the road—and impose them on those who reject them.[9]

What side will win today's struggle? What will be the enduring and defining character of our world? Will society triumph over anarchy? And, if so, what kind of society will that be? If it is too soon to answer such questions, it is not too soon to assert that the most influential factor will be the actions of the United States—the "hyperpower," in the words of Hubert Vedrine, a former foreign minister of France.

Integrating the World

WHAT IS IT THE United States should be doing? The United States should be using its power and influence to persuade the major powers of the day, along with as many other countries, organizations, corporations, and individuals as possible, to sign up to and support a set of rules, policies, and institutions that would bring about a world in which armed conflict between and within states is the exception; where terrorists find it difficult to succeed; where the spread of weapons of mass destruction is halted and ultimately reversed; in which markets are open to goods and services and in which societies are free and open to ideas; and where the world's people have a good chance to live out lives of normal span free from violence, extreme poverty, and deadly disease. Our policies must recognize that globalization is a reality, not a choice. As Prime Minister Tony Blair has stated, "We are all internationalists now, whether we like it or not."[10] But what to do about globalization, how to contend with it, does involve choice. The choice before the United States is between an effective multilateralism and either a gradual return to a world of great power competition or a world overwhelmed by disruptive forces, or both.

To have a chance of succeeding, the United States will need to view other major powers less as rivals and more as partners. Much the same applies to relations with critical medium powers such as Brazil in South America, South Africa and Nigeria in Africa, and South Korea and Australia in East Asia. The United States will have to accept some constraints on its freedom of action. It will have to make a concerted effort to build international consensus on the principles and rules that ought to govern international relations. It will have to use all the foreign policy tools at its disposal and not only or even mostly the military. It will have to get more involved in reforming other societies. Americans will need to rethink some of their traditional ideas about sovereignty. In all of this, the United States will not be able to simply impose its preferences. Power is not the same as influence; to the contrary, power is better understood as potential. The goal of foreign policy is to translate this potential into lasting influence.

There is a precedent for trying to bring about a world in which the leading states of the day do often act as partners. In the early nineteenth century, the major powers of the era met in Vienna and subsequently in other cities to develop understandings—rules of the road, in today's parlance—about the conduct of international relations. The goal was to devise "international agreement about the nature of workable arrangements and about the permissible aims and methods of foreign policy."[11] While more modest than that, the resulting "Concert of Europe" helped to keep relative peace for several decades among the great powers—Austria, Britain, France, Prussia, and Russia—then at the heart of the European state system. The arrangements were never institutionalized, much less codified as some form of world government; rather, what emerged were a set of understandings and a commitment to consult in order to avoid the sort of major power conflict Europe had just experienced (the Napoleonic Wars), in large part leaving all five governments better able to contend with the rising pressures for self-determination and greater freedom and opportunity that threatened a world of empires and hereditary elites.[12]

This period following the Congress of Vienna is not the only example of coordination among the major powers of the day. More recently, the Cold War was kept cold (as opposed to going hot) by a series of implicit or informal understandings between the United States and the Soviet Union.[13] Both had a stake in avoiding a nuclear conflict that neither could win; as a result, each avoided any direct armed intervention against the other on the grounds that escalation to nuclear war was all too possible. In addition, it was acceptable to provide military assistance to an ally or client, but not to the point of overwhelming the ally or client of the other. The most dangerous moments of the Cold War came when such "rules" were violated or came close to being violated.

Rules of the road are just as necessary in the contemporary era. What is needed, though, are not simply "negative" understandings among the major powers that constrain competition, but "positive" commitments about how to work together to meet pressing challenges. The challenge is not simply to erect an international society with commonly accepted restraints but to fashion coalitions and institutions that promote certain objectives sought by the United States and embraced by others.

Areas for potential cooperation include what to do with

governments that either commit genocide against their own citizens or are so weak that they cannot prevent massacres from occurring. Another is how to prevent (or revive) failed states. There is as well the matter of how best to promote open societies and open markets and reduce poverty, disease, and emissions that contribute to global climate change. Also needed is cooperation against terrorism, including rules to prohibit state support of terrorism. And, arguably most important, it is essential that the powers of the day work together to slow or better yet stop the spread of weapons of mass destruction, above all nuclear weapons.

History and realist theory suggest that such talk of sustained international cooperation is unrealistic and that it is only a matter of time before one or more of these major actors (most likely China or an increasingly united and alienated Europe) challenges American primacy.[14] But this is by no means inevitable. Countries tend to challenge the status quo when they see it as being inconsistent with their national aspirations and vulnerable to challenge. The objective for U.S. foreign policy should be to persuade others to work with the United States—and to persuade them that it is neither wise to work against the United States, given its strength, nor necessary to work against it, given its intentions.

The administration of George W. Bush has it half right when it comes to this point. It has stressed the importance of maintaining a U.S. power advantage that would discourage challengers. "The United States must and will maintain the capability to defeat any attempt by an enemy—whether a state or non-state actor—to impose its will on the United States, our allies, or our friends. . . . Our forces will be strong enough to dissuade potential adversaries from pursuing a military build-up in hopes of surpassing, or equaling, the power of the United States."[15]

There are limits to this approach, however. The United States is not in a position to prevent the rise of other powers. The rise and decline of states has a great deal to do with demographics, culture, natural resources, educational systems, economic policy, political stability, individual opportunity, legal frameworks—all matters largely beyond the control of outsiders. Put another way, there is not a lot the United States could do to prevent the rise of either China or Russia or India or Europe—any more than Europe was able to prevent the rise of the United States in the nineteenth and twentieth centuries. Any effort on the part of the United States to frustrate the rise of another country would guarantee that government's animosity and all but ensure its working against U.S. efforts around the world.

Nor should the United States want to discourage the emergence of strong countries; to the contrary, the United States needs other countries to be strong if it is to have the partners it requires to meet the challenges posed by globalization. The issue for American foreign policy should not be whether China becomes strong, but rather *how* China uses its growing strength. The same point applies to India, Brazil,

South Korea, South Africa, and others. The United States should also encourage the emergence of a more unified and stronger Europe, as such a Europe has the potential to be a valuable partner in addressing global challenges. And the United States should favor the gradual "normalization" of Japanese foreign policy; only a Japan that sheds many of its post–World II constraints can play a significant role in contributing to the stability of Asia and in assisting war-torn societies.

It is not enough, though, to discourage major power competition or conflict. U.S. foreign policy needs to encourage cooperation. Even if other countries choose not to challenge the United States directly, they could elect to sit on their hands; for the immediate future, noncooperation is likely to be a more frequent and a bigger problem for U.S. foreign policy than direct opposition. The costly and damaging consequences of noncooperation are visible in postwar Iraq: For more than two years, few governments proved willing to commit troops or resources to assist that country's new leaders and its people recover from decades of tyranny and the more recent war and subsequent disorder. Over time, this kind of passive resistance on the part of other major powers to U.S. policies abroad will drain the resources of the United States or lead to less effective international action against contemporary challenges, or both. Everyone will be worse off.

As a result, the goal of U.S. foreign policy should not simply be to maintain a world defined by U.S. military superiority. Rather, the priority for American foreign policy should be to integrate other states into American-sponsored or American-supported efforts to deal with the challenges of globalization. This can only be achieved through consent, not coercion. As Henry Kissinger has correctly noted, "American power is a fact of life, but the art of diplomacy is to translate power into consensus."[16]

Consent, in turn, presupposes a common view of what constitutes legitimate behavior. American foreign policy, then, should aim to promote a shared definition of legitimacy among the major powers and others, one that reflects a shared view of the proper ends and means of international relations. Against such a common backdrop, it would be possible to integrate other countries and organizations into arrangements that could sustain a world consistent with U.S. interests and values—interests and values that are in no way narrowly or uniquely American. Integration of new partners into U.S. efforts worldwide will help the United States deal with traditional challenges of maintaining peace in divided regions and protecting vulnerable populations as well as with meeting transnational threats such as international terrorism and the proliferation of weapons of mass destruction. It will also help bring into the modern world those billions of people living in dozens of countries who have largely missed out on the benefits of open markets and political systems, a development that would be good in and of itself for humanitarian reasons but which would likely have desirable economic and strategic dividends as well.

"Integration" is a word that brings to mind certain images, most often those associated with efforts to bring about a society in which race or religion do not define individual rights or access to services. In its most basic sense, however, it entails the combining or incorporating of parts into a larger whole.

An American foreign policy based upon a doctrine of integration would have three dimensions. First, it would aim to create a cooperative relationship among the world's major powers—a twenty-first-century concert—built on a common commitment to promoting certain principles and outcomes. Second, it would seek to translate this commitment into effective arrangements and actions. Third, it would work to bring in other countries, organizations, and peoples so that they come to enjoy the benefits of physical security, economic opportunity, and political freedom. The goal would be to create a more integrated world both in the sense of integrating (involving) as many governments and organizations and societies as possible and in the sense of bringing about a more integrated (cooperative) international community so that the challenges central to the modern era could better be met.

Integration is the natural successor to containment, which was the necessary and correct policy construct for the Cold War. Containment—in George Kennan's formulation, "a commitment to countering the Soviet Union wherever it encroached upon the interests of a peaceful and stable world"—implicitly and correctly rejected two dangerous alternatives: appeasement of the Soviet and Communist threat on the one hand, something that would have led to a diminution of security and freedom and prosperity around the world, and direct confrontation on the other, something that would have been all too dangerous in a nuclear era.[17]

Containment, which survived some four decades of Soviet challenge, could not, however, survive its own success. What is needed as a result is a foreign policy doctrine for both a post-11/9 (November 9, 1989, when the Berlin Wall came down, signifying the Cold War's end) and a post-9/11 world. A doctrine relevant to this era, however, would seek to bring others in, not keep them out. That a guiding principle is needed cannot be doubted. An intellectual framework furnishes policymakers with a compass to determine priorities, which in turn help shape decisions affecting long-term investments involving military forces, assistance programs, and both intelligence and diplomatic assets. A doctrine also helps prepare the public for what may be required—and sends signals to other governments, groups, and individuals (friend and foe alike) about what the country is striving to seek or prevent in the world.

None of three post–Cold War presidencies has successfully articulated a comprehensive foreign policy or national security doctrine. The first Bush administration spoke of a "New World Order" but never defined it. The Clinton administration wrote of enlarging the circle of democracies but never put this enterprise at the center of a consistent foreign policy. Attempts to ascribe a "Bush Doctrine" to the first term of George W. Bush came up short, as there was less a coherent policy than a mix of counterterrorism, democracy promotion, preemption, and unilateralism.[18]

The opportunity exists for our era to become one of genuine global integration. More than any other alternative, integration offers a coherent response to globalization and to the transnational threats that constitute the defining challenges of the era. Ruled out, then, as a national security doctrine is unilateralism. No single country, no matter how powerful, can contend successfully on its own with transnational challenges. Any such effort will fail. It will also have two other adverse consequences: It will stimulate the reemergence of a world defined by a balance of power, and it will erode the economic (and possibly political and military) foundations of U.S. strength that are in part responsible for the opportunity that now exists.[19]

None of this should be construed as an argument against American leadership. But leadership implies followership. Unilateralism is just that: acting alone. Most of today's pressing problems cannot be met by the United States alone, given the nature of the problems themselves and the realistic limits to American power. To take just one example, critical foreign policy tools such as sanctions will have little impact unless other potential partners of a target government join the United States in a policy of isolation.

The administration of George W. Bush is fond of saying that the United States needs no permission slip from the United Nations or anybody else to act.[20] This is true. No country and certainly no great power would or should allow itself to be so hamstrung. But this in no way negates the point that the United States can only achieve what it seeks in the world if others work with it as opposed to against it or not at all. In the end, the United States does not need the world's permission to act, but it does need the world's support to succeed.

Isolationism is no better as an alternative. No country can escape the consequences of globalization. It is not simply that there is no hiding from globalization; it is also that the world cannot be expected to sort itself out without leadership, something only the United States can provide right now. Unlike Adam Smith's economic model, there is no invisible hand ensuring that all works out for the best in the geopolitical marketplace.

Counterterrorism alone does not constitute an adequate foreign policy ambition for the United States. It is too narrow in scope and provides no guidance for dealing with a majority of the opportunities and challenges posed by globalization and international relations. Moreover, the surest way to address the threat of terrorism is integration. Only by integrating other countries into the struggle against existing and potential terrorism can the United States succeed.

Promoting democracy is another potential foreign policy lodestar, one that appears to be the preferred approach of the second term of George W. Bush. "America's vital interests and our deepest beliefs are now one," the president proclaimed in his second inaugural address. "So it is the policy of the United States to seek and support the growth of democratic movements and institutions in every nation and culture, with the ultimate goal of ending tyranny in our world. . . . We will encourage reform in other governments by making clear that success in our relations will require the decent treatment of their own people. America's belief in human dignity will guide our policies."

It is, however, neither desirable nor practical to make democracy promotion a foreign policy doctrine. Too many pressing threats in which the lives of millions hang in the balance—from dealing with today's terrorists and managing Iranian and North Korean nuclear capabilities to coping with protectionism and genocide—will not be solved by the emergence of democracy. Promoting democracy is and should be one foreign policy goal, but it cannot be the only or dominant objective. When it comes to relations with Russia or China, other national security interests must normally take precedence over concerns about how they choose to govern themselves. The fact that promoting democracy can be difficult and expensive also reduces its attraction as a foreign policy compass.[21]

Integration can be a bold, transforming strategy by which the United States can shape the next era of history. This is an optimistic prospect, but one more modest in imagination than, say, someone writing amid World War II of a Europe in which Franco-German friendship is the cornerstone, or of someone writing in 1951 (the year I was born) of a post–Cold War, post-Soviet world in which markets and democracies are more the world's rule than an exception. An integrated world can, with American guidance, become an achievable reality.

Some will see a risk that integration might prove too successful: Following an extended period of international calm, a much stronger China or Europe might then turn on the United States. Some analysts take such a risk seriously: "[T]he United States has a profound interest in seeing Chinese economic growth slow considerably in the years ahead. . . . A wealthy China would not be a status quo power but an aggressive state determined to achieve regional hegemony."[22] Here again, though, the strategy of integration offers reassurance. At its core is the ambition to give other powers a substantial stake in the maintenance of order—in effect, to co-opt them and make them pillars of international society—so that they will come to see it in their self-interest to continue working with the United States and damaging to their interests to have a falling-out with the United States. We are far more likely to face a disruptive major power down the road if we do not pursue the idea of integration.

This will not always be easy, particularly given the level of anti-Americanism that currently exists. It would be wrong, however, to view today's sentiments as representing what might be described as a strategic choice by governments to counter the efforts of the United States throughout the world. Although some anti-Americanism can be attributed to natural resentment of a stronger country, the bulk of anti-American sentiment stems from disagreement over particular U.S. policies, especially the war against Iraq, the Palestinian issue and the perception in many quarters of uncritical U.S. support for Israel, and U.S. rejection of multiple international arrangements. The style and tone of American foreign policy during the first term of George W. Bush's presidency has also had an impact. But much of today's anti-Americanism need not be either structural or permanent. It is essential that policies and how they are promoted be adjusted. Anti-Americanism makes it more difficult for the United States to find useful and at times necessary partners. Even worse, over time, the perception that Americans do not have a decent respect for the opinions of mankind could bring to power individuals and governments around the world who view the United States as a threat that needs to be countered.

The current period is not the first time the United States has emerged from a major war blessed with great power and the opportunity to make the world more secure, prosperous, and in general, better off.[23] Following World War I, the United States (and both France and Great Britain) could and should have done much more to prevent the rise of German power that over the course of two decades led to World War II. A foreign policy that does too little can be as dangerous as one that aims to do too much.

Even more, though, the current period resembles the era

just following World War II. Then, as now, the United States emerged from years of intense struggle as the most powerful country in the world. Then, as now, the United States emerged triumphant from one struggle only to face another. Then, as now, the United States needed partners in order to meet the new set of challenges it faced. It did so after World War II in an extraordinary fashion; for good reason did Dean Acheson, President Harry S. Truman's secretary of state, title his memoirs *Present at the Creation*. It truly was a creative time, one that gave rise to the United Nations, the North Atlantic Treaty Organization (NATO), the International Monetary Fund (IMF), the World Bank, the General Agreement on Tariffs and Trade (or GATT, the precursor to the World Trade Organization [WTO]), theories and polices of nuclear deterrence, and, in the United States, the national security council system and a modern intelligence community.

The obvious question is whether the United States will prove to be equally creative now. This is a time for new thinking: about sovereignty, about how to view other major powers, about the purposes of foreign policy. It is also a time for new programs and arrangements: to contend better with terrorism, to stem the spread of nuclear weapons, to decrease the number of innocent people around the world at risk from internal conflicts and disease, to help the Arab world modernize its societies so it no longer produces legions of alienated young men and women all too eager to die rather than live for their causes.

All of which brings us back to the fundamental argument of this book, that of opportunity. The question is what Americans and others make of this moment. Time, resources, and potential have already been squandered. A different foreign policy, one based on promoting the world's integration while the opportunity to do so still exists, is urgently necessary.

2

●

A Little Less Sovereignty

THE ATTEMPT TO construct a more integrated world does not have to begin from scratch. A degree of international society, even a degree of concert, already exists. Contemporary international relations are not some all-out, unregulated struggle; to the contrary, there are some important principles that are widely embraced, and in some areas these principles are buttressed by institutional arrangements. In short, the world is already somewhat integrated and, in some areas such as trade, quite significantly so (see integration index).

There is, for example, near-universal support for the right of self-defense, the concept that a state can respond militarily if attacked. This right is enshrined in Article 51 of the UN Charter, which explicitly states: "Nothing . . . shall impair the inherent right of individual or collective self-defense if an armed attack occurs against a Member of the United Nations. . . ." As the text makes clear, the notion of self-defense applies not simply to the state under attack but also provides a mechanism for other parties to come to the defense of the victim. All this was embraced by Kuwait, and subsequently by the international community, in the aftermath of the August 1990 Iraqi invasion and occupation of its wealthy but small and relatively weak neighbor.

In the realm of security, there is a host of arms control agreements that place ceilings on or eliminate entire categories of armaments, as well as so-called laws of war that influence when and how military force is to be used, including what governments are obligated to do to safeguard the rights of combatants and noncombatants alike.

There are elements of a consensus in the political realm, including a number of international conventions supporting human rights and democracy and opposing torture, slavery, and genocide. The United Nations, despite its weaknesses and shortcomings, is an institution of some— and, at times, considerable—international authority. Other groupings that contribute in meaningful ways to international cooperation include the G-8 (consisting of Canada, France, Germany, Italy, Japan, Russia, and the United Kingdom in addition to the United States) and many of the numerous regional organizations (the African Union [AU], the Organization of American States [OAS], the Association of Southeast Asian Nations [ASEAN], and above all the European Union) that reflect a degree of consensus about not just local but also international matters. Transatlantic arrangements, including NATO, also contribute meaningfully to political order in the world.

Technical arrangements abound when it comes to issues

that affect the ability to function efficiently in a global world. Aviation safety standards, communications conventions, and international rules affecting agricultural and health policies have become essential for facilitating international travel, broadcasting, trade, and safety. In the environmental realm, there is also a considerable degree of integration, in particular international arrangements with near-universal participation that protect the ozone layer and ban persistent organic pollutants. Most of the world's countries participate in the UN Framework Convention on Climate Change, while all of the major powers other than the United States have ratified and agreed to implement the Kyoto Protocol.

There are many examples of significant cooperation in the economic realm. Even a partial list would include the World Trade Organization, the International Monetary Fund and the World Bank, the Paris Club for debt rescheduling, the G-7 group of leading industrialized countries (essentially, the G-8 minus Russia), the Bank for International Settlements, the International Energy Agency (IEA) (designed to help oil-importing countries weather a supply interruption), and the Organization for Economic Cooperation and Development (OECD).

In principle, an integrated international system could consist of any number of arrangements and shared objectives in addition to the ones just listed. A modern-day concert could be premised on opposition to terrorism, the spread of weapons of mass destruction in general and nu-

clear weapons and materials in particular, and both genocide and all forms of severe repression such as ethnic
cleansing. It could also encompass support for free trade
and economic openness, democracy and human rights,
economic development and the raising of living standards
for the world's poor, and efforts to combat global climate
change as well as the spread of HIV/AIDS and other infectious diseases.

Why these objectives and not others? Although the list
is both subjective and selective, it represents those goals
that, if realized, would have the greatest positive impact on
the security, prosperity, and quality of life of the countries
and peoples of the world. It is not meant to be exclusive;
indeed, if there were progress in these areas, it would suggest a degree of commonality of thinking among today's
major powers and readiness to work with others that would
almost certainly make progress possible in other areas.

Four areas in particular show both the immediate benefit that integration might deliver as well as highlighting
some significant obstacles: opposing genocide, stopping
terrorism, stemming the spread of weapons of mass destruction, and promoting open trade. Each is of great importance, and some degree of support for each objective
exists among the major powers, as does the potential for
more.

Making progress on these four goals would, however, require a degree of new thinking. The four have in common
a somewhat different (or, more precisely, limited) approach

to state sovereignty that, if embraced, would constitute an important departure from international relations as we have known it.

Sovereignty is a central building block of modern international relations. Only states enjoy sovereignty. It is states that have rights and roles, dominate international gatherings, and are members of the United Nations and other international organizations. What, though, makes a state sovereign? In theory, a state qualifies as sovereign if it meets four criteria. First, a sovereign state is meant to enjoy supreme political authority and a monopoly on the legitimate use of force within its borders. Second, a sovereign state is supposed to be able to control its borders and regulate what goes in and out of its territory. Third, a sovereign state is free to adopt the foreign and domestic policies it wants. And fourth, a sovereign state is one so recognized by its peers.

In reality, the test for sovereignty is more lenient. State sovereignty has always been less than absolute in practice. Governments continued to try to influence "domestic" developments in other countries, at times for reasons of high principle (say, to promote freedom), at other times more for reasons of relatively low politics (to weaken a rival from within). Smugglers and others often cross borders with impunity, as do multinational corporations.

The "balance of power" in international relations overwhelmingly favors states and governments. In recent years, however, this balance has begun to evolve. More than anything else, it is the nature of globalization that explains this change. States cannot regulate much of what flows across their borders in ever-increasing volume and with ever-increasing velocity. In addition, there has been an explosion in the number of entities active in more than one country. As well as multinational corporations, millions of non-governmental organizations (NGOs) exist around the world. One analyst summed all this up as constituting a "power shift" in the world, one in which states and governments increasingly have to share the stage with other non-sovereign entities that possess real independence, power, and influence.[1] Each has taken away a little of the state's sovereign authority. In this respect, the emergence of these entities anticipated a future in which state sovereignty *needs* to become somewhat weaker in selected areas in order to protect the interests of most people and countries in the world, including Americans and the United States.

This is not to confuse the world we are entering with the relatively unstructured world that existed some four centuries ago, just before state sovereignty first became the norm. Until that time, it was commonplace for states to meddle in the affairs of their neighbors, a practice that often resulted in wider conflict. (The "Dark Ages" are described as "dark" for a reason.) After the Thirty Years' War, Europe's leaders accepted the notion (in the 1648 Treaty of Westphalia) that each ruler was to respect what might be described as the internal independence of the others; in return, the rulers enjoyed a "right" to act pretty much as they pleased within their own borders. Such collective restraint contributed to greater international stability; the widespread adoption of the notion of sovereignty constituted a major development in the emergence of what Hedley Bull would term "international society." Who would want to abandon that?

Americans have traditionally guarded their sovereignty with more than a little ferocity. There is a long tradition of suspecting entangling alliances, the United Nations, and, more recently, the International Criminal Court (ICC). Nevertheless, the world requires (and the United States would benefit from) a concept of state sovereignty that is less than absolute. To be precise, it would benefit from a concept of state sovereignty that is contractual, one that recognizes the obligations and responsibilities as well as the rights of those who enjoy it. Such an approach to sovereignty would essentially communicate to governments and their leaders that the rights and protections they associate with statehood are in fact conditional and that governments and leaders would forfeit some or, in extreme cases, all of these rights and protections if they acted in contravention of certain norms or rules. "Abuse it and lose it" would make for a good bumper sticker.[2]

Now that borders are porous, every country is or can be affected by what goes on inside other states. To paraphrase John Donne (and setting aside the geography of Japan, Indonesia, the Philippines, Sri Lanka, Haiti, Cuba, and Madagascar, among others), no country is an island. The notion that the world is somehow divided into internal and external spheres and that foreign policy and national security policies of the United States (or any country for that matter) need or can only deal with the external and can safely ignore the internal or domestic side of other countries is an anachronism. We live in an age in which what takes place inside one country can easily affect developments within another. This is true whether one is talking about disease, terrorists, weapons, or jobs. U.S. foreign policy needs to concern itself with the domestic policies of others; it is essential to adopt an approach to international relations that takes all this into account.

Humanitarian Intervention

THIS IDEA THAT foreign policy ought to concern itself more with what takes place inside other countries is anything but academic. It has far-ranging consequences for the world in several ways. One involves situations of genocide or severe repression in one country, in many ways the dominant foreign policy issue of the 1990s. Somalia, Bosnia, Kosovo, Haiti, Rwanda, East Timor—all involved situations where large numbers of innocent civilians were placed at risk from threats largely or entirely emanating from within their own borders.

Conventional wisdom would argue that these conflicts were not of foreign policy or national security concern. But in addition to the fact that there is something morally wrong in looking the other way when fellow human beings are being slaughtered, that we are all our brother's keeper and have some basic obligation to one another, there are "strategic" reasons that justify concern. Massive human rights violations tend to create large refugee flows that can pose a severe economic and political cost on neighboring countries and can on occasion trigger a wider war, such as the 1971 South Asia crisis that led to war between India and Pakistan and that became midwife to the independent country of Bangladesh (formerly East Pakistan). Countries with severe internal unrest can all too easily become weak and in the process vulnerable to terrorist groups that set up shop free of central government interference. Over time, what begins as or appears to be "simply" a humanitarian crisis can in fact be or become much more.

Effective international action requires an appreciation that sovereignty is not absolute and that citizens as well as governments have rights. Governments should not be allowed to massacre their own people. Weak governments should not be allowed to permit massacres to take place on their own territory even if they are not themselves the perpetrator. The act of genocide is proof that the state has failed in its duty to its citizens. It should, as a result, forfeit some or all of its sovereignty.

None of this is particularly new. What is new, though, is the idea that the major powers and the international community more broadly would go beyond embracing this principle and accept the necessary consequence: that other states and the international community at large have a right and a duty to act to protect innocent life when it is jeopardized on a large scale.

Intervention in such circumstances can take any number of forms, from public rhetoric and private diplomacy to economic and political sanctions to armed intervention. When it comes to the use of military force, the goal can be to protect an endangered population (as was initially done in Somalia in 1991), to coerce a government until behavior or policy is altered (as in the bombing of Serbia to force it to stay its hand in Kosovo), or even to overthrow a regime. This became the objective in Somalia when the Clinton administration determined that the removal of Mohammed Farah Aideed was essential. It was used as well as a rationale for the 2003 war against Iraq, although it was by no means the original or principal reason for the U.S. action. Ideally, the government in question would accept (and not physically resist) an international intervention (as Haiti did in 1994 and Indonesia did in the case of East Timor in 2000), but this cannot be a prerequisite, especially given that in these two cases government consent came only after the United States in the first instance and Australia in the second appeared prepared to enter its territory with or without an invitation. The challenge, then, is to define when an outside agency can reasonably intervene in the internal affairs of a nation-state.

There is quite a lot to build on; a degree of integration

exists. The Universal Declaration of Human Rights asserts (among other things) that all humans are born free and equal, regardless of race, color, sex, religion, politics, or status; that slavery is to be prohibited in all forms; and that no one should be subjected to torture or to cruel, inhuman, or degrading treatment. The Convention on the Prevention and Punishment of the Crime of Genocide confirms that genocide is a crime under international law and that those states signing the convention undertake to prevent it and, failing that, punish those who commit it.

There is also some case history. The idea that states should not massacre their own or allow their own to be massacred was at the core of the American and European response to the tragedies in the Balkans in the 1990s. The intervention was premised on the notion that Serbian president Slobodan Milosevic should not be allowed to carry out wide-scale ethnic cleansing, much less murder, of his own populations, that sovereignty did not confer upon him that right. Related to this conclusion was the notion that the international community had the right to act if a state failed to meet its obligation to protect its own people, as Serbia did first in Bosnia and then in Kosovo.

There is growing support (mostly in the United States and much of Europe) for the legitimacy of intervention undertaken for humanitarian reasons. British prime minister Tony Blair articulated such a view in April 1999: "[T]he principle of non-interference must be qualified in important respects. Acts of genocide can never be a purely internal matter. When oppression produces massive flows of refugees which unsettle neighboring countries then they can properly be described as 'threats to international peace and security.'"[3]

However, the Kosovo experience also demonstrates that this concept is not universally embraced. Neither Russia nor China was prepared to support international action against the government of Serbia (or on behalf of Serbian citizens) without a request from the Serbian government. In December 1999, Russia and China issued a joint statement calling upon others to "fully respect the sovereignty and territorial integrity of Yugoslavia [and] observe the UN Charter and generally recognized principles of international law," much of which is code for opposing military action against a state for what it does vis-à-vis its own citizens.[4]

What appeared to motivate both countries was concern that they would be setting or reinforcing a precedent that the international community did in fact possess the right to intervene in matters traditionally viewed as falling within the sovereign purview of an independent country. Apparently, both China and Russia feared that this principle could be used against them, be it to limit Russia's freedom of action in Chechnya or to limit what China could do in territory that it claims as its own, such as Tibet or Taiwan. India had similar worries, stemming from its claims to Kashmir. The net result is that the United States and Europe could not garner UN Security Council backing for any armed intervention in Kosovo and instead shifted their diplomatic efforts to Brussels, where they could get NATO to provide a more limited but still multilateral "authorization" for armed action as well as the means to carry it out.

The challenge for the United States is to integrate those who see humanitarian intervention as a pretext for military action. This will not be easy; a statement by the Shanghai Cooperation Organization (a group consisting of China, Russia, and four Central Asian countries, formed in 2000 to promote stability in that region) specifically opposed "interference into the internal affairs of other states, including under the pretext of humanitarian intervention."[5] To the extent that Chinese, Russian, and Indian reluctance to cooperate with the United States and Europe in this area is based on fear that their own sovereignty will be undermined, the U.S. government and the EU should reassure them that this new thinking is not a challenge to their claims to Tibet, Chechnya, and Kashmir, respectively. To persuade others of the wisdom of adopting a new approach will also require making clear that the threshold for armed intervention is high: A large number of people (thousands or more) must be in life-threatening danger, other policies must be shown to promise little or no remedy, and a strong case must be made that military force is likely to have a meaningful impact.[6]

There is, however, the danger of setting the standard too high: hundreds of thousands of innocent lives have been lost or made miserable while the world debated whether what was taking place in Rwanda or in the Darfur area of Sudan actually constituted genocide. The international community needs to move away from the unhelpful language of the Genocide Convention, which requires a finding of "*intent* to destroy, in whole or in part, a national, ethnical, racial, or religious group," as an essential trigger for acting. What should dictate the international response is what is taking place rather than proof of intent, something often difficult to demonstrate. All forms of intervention, and not just the military, must be considered. So-called smart sanctions targeted against the financial holdings of leaders or their ability to travel can be useful, as can the threat of war crimes trials. Consensus on these points would represent an important accomplishment: It would at least hold open the prospect of major power action, something that in turn might help dissuade leaders from undertaking or continuing policies that place populations at risk.

In the instance of Darfur, to take one example, what is needed from the outside world is massive assistance to displaced persons so that those who survive conflict do not succumb to disease and starvation. Diplomatic efforts are required to bring about a cease-fire and, following that, a settlement that addresses the grievances that helped bring about the crisis in the first place. In addition, countries including the United States should provide the relevant regional body—in this case the African Union—with the logistical, material, and financial help it has requested. With such support, AU-authorized troops could guard the refugee camps and, over time, protect villages so that men, women, and children could return home in safety. And the international community ought to impose sanctions against the Sudanese government unless it stops using its aircraft to destroy villages and unless it stops supporting the Jangaweed, the Arab fighters on horseback who raid villages with the intent of emptying them through murder and rape. Criminal indictments for war crimes ought to be issued against specific officials who do not comply.

Beyond Darfur, what is required is a far greater number of police and military forces with training and skills appropriate for these difficult situations. Most of these forces need not (and arguably should not) come from the major powers, whose motives may be questioned and who by their very strength can stimulate nationalist resistance to a foreign presence. By contrast, regional forces can have a greater incentive to act and often possess similar language skills and greater familiarity with local situations.

A measure of how much progress has been made in moving international thinking about humanitarian intervention is the basic document ("Constitutive Act") of the African Union, the regional organization launched in July 2000 to replace the ineffective Organization of African Unity. After citing the principle of noninterference by one member state in the internal affairs of another, the document goes on to declare "the right of the Union to intervene in a member state pursuant to a decision of the assembly [where all member states are represented] in respect of grave circumstances, namely war crimes, genocide and crimes against humanity." The significance of this intellectual and political departure should not be underestimated, given that the UN Charter (in Article 2) explicitly states that member states should "refrain in their international relations from the threat or use of force against the territorial integrity or political independence of any state. . . ."

Here lies the opportunity. The world is increasingly embracing two notions that only recently would have been widely regarded as radical: that sovereignty is not absolute, and that outside intervention is not always undesirable or a threat to order. To the contrary, the view is taking hold that in certain circumstances outside intervention is a necessity, both to preserve life and to preserve the peace. What is needed is the willingness of outsiders, including the United States, Europe, and Japan, to intervene or, more commonly, to fund, train, equip, and support regional forces prepared to do the difficult work of intervention in such circumstances. Put differently, the real issue is increasingly one of policy rather than principle. This is progress by any standard.

3

•

Taking On Terrorism

AN ESSENTIAL obligation of sovereignty is that governments should neither support terrorism—the intentional killing of innocent men, women, and children by actors other than states for political purposes—nor allow their territory or their resources to be used by those who do. If a state does such a thing or actively promotes or permits it to occur from its territory, it is an act of war. But terrorism can also happen without state support, either because of state weakness (the state is not strong enough to deny use of its territory by some group) or government ignorance of what is actually going on.

The goal of American foreign policy, then, ought to be to get wide acceptance of the notion that no form of purposeful killing of innocents is permissible in today's world. Branding terrorism as wrong is important. It does not matter whether people believed differently in the past or that some uses of terror were or are judged by some people to have been justified at the time. Making sure that terrorism and support for it are viewed as illegitimate is the equivalent of calling for the abolition of slavery. Modern terror is too destructive to be tolerated. The world needs to agree to this. After that consensus is reached, governments can argue in the specific case about what to do. But without such a consensus, it will be far more difficult if not impossible to forge a common policy.

Significant progress is being made. There is considerable international agreement that terrorism is not to be condoned or supported in any way. The major powers are all parties to a dozen international conventions and have voted for numerous UN resolutions that oppose the taking of hostages, the hijacking of civilian aircraft, and terrorism more broadly. The Financial Action Task Force, created in 1989 to curb money laundering, has seen its mandate greatly expanded so that it is now focused on curbing terrorist financing. UN Security Council Resolution 1373, passed in the aftermath of the September 11 attacks, lays out a number of steps all states should take to block financing of terrorist acts and calls on states to deny safe haven to terrorists, bring to justice anyone associated with terrorism, suppress recruitment by terrorist groups, block efforts by terrorists to acquire weapons, and cooperate with other governments and international organizations so that terrorists find it more difficult to carry on with their work. This same resolution also established a UN Counter-Terrorism Committee to monitor implementation of anti-terrorism commitments. A good deal of intelligence sharing and law enforcement cooperation has also grown up between and among states. All this is evidence of integration in action.

On one recent occasion, widespread support was expressed for the legitimacy of acting against a government that actively supported terrorism. The idea that states ought not to be in the business of terrorism was at the core of the U.S.-led ouster of the Taliban from Afghanistan. The Taliban did not carry out 9/11. There were no Afghans among the nineteen terrorists on the planes that killed 3,000 innocent people. But it was the Taliban that allowed Afghanistan to be the base for al Qaeda. The international community rallied around the United States (passing UN Security Council Resolution 1378 of November 14, 2001, by a unanimous vote) when it sought backing to oust the Taliban-controlled Afghan government in the wake of the 9/11 terrorist attacks.

It would be a mistake, though, to conclude that there is global consensus on this matter. There is not, in part because of disagreement over what constitutes terrorism. The definition of terrorism used here—the purposeful killing of noncombatants and civilians by nonstate actors for political purposes—would not necessarily be everyone else's. As the old adage goes, one man's terrorist is another man's freedom fighter. Here again, though, there seems to be progress, as the December 2004 report of the UN High-Level Panel commissioned by Secretary-General Kofi Annan explicitly stated that "there is nothing in the fact of occupation that justifies the targeting and killing of civilians" and recommended that a definition of terrorism be adopted that would rule out the ends ever justifying it as a means.[1]

The greater challenge is to agree on the correct remedy when terrorism is carried out by a state or a state allows its territory to be used by terrorists. In many instances, the United States has found itself mostly on its own when it has sought to build international support for politically and economically sanctioning those governments (most notably North Korea, Iran, Syria, and Cuba) it considers to be state sponsors of terror. (The United States did do better when it came to garnering international support for sanctions against Libya, but this may have been because Libyan-sponsored terrorism affected France and the United Kingdom directly.) There is also disagreement (especially in Europe) as to the wisdom of economic sanctions as a tool. Broad sanctions can penalize the same people on whose behalf they have been invoked. Sanctions can also have the perverse effect of reinforcing central authority by requiring that all economic activity go through limited and often government-controlled channels.[2]

Still, there is far greater international cooperation against terrorism than before. All of the other major powers have had their own painful experience with terrorism, which reinforces the perception that terrorism constitutes a common threat requiring a collective response. The recognition seems to be growing that terrorism can no longer be justified or tolerated whatever the cause, given the vulnerability of modern societies and the killing potential of modern weapons. The goal should be to codify this emerging consensus in a new international convention that would define terror and put countries on record to deny terrorists support of any kind.

As useful as such an agreement would be, international efforts to delegitimize terrorism and deny terrorists financial resources or safe haven or ever more powerful weapons, while essential, are not enough. Terrorism turns out to be not just terrible but terribly complex. Speaking of a "war on terrorism," however, does not help to define either the threat or the solution. Wars tend to be fought with military arms by soldiers on battlefields. None of this applies to terrorism. Terrorists use box cutters, civilian aircraft, parked cars, and trucks. For terrorists there is no battlefield—or every place is a battlefield, from airports and shopping malls to restaurants and movie theaters.

Also, wars have an end. Although they range from the Six Days' War in the Middle East in 1967 to the Thirty Years' War some three centuries before in Europe to the Hundred Years' War between England and France, wars usually have discernible beginnings and endings, often ratified by a treaty. But there is unlikely to be any end to the war on terrorism. There will always be individuals and groups with a grievance or a set of objectives that they believe gives them the license to kill and destroy. The fact that terrorists belong to no single organization only compounds the problem. Osama bin Laden could be captured or killed, al Qaeda could disappear, but offshoots would live on. Indeed, Osama bin Laden can in some ways be understood as a foundation president who provides resources and guidance to largely independent groups. As one U.S. government report published in 2003 realistically stated: "Victory against terrorism will not occur in a single, defining moment. It will not be marked by the likes of a surrender ceremony on the deck of the USS *Missouri* that ended World War II."[3]

So if terrorism is not a war, how should we understand it? Perhaps as a disease. There are steps that can be taken to eradicate or neutralize specific viruses or bacteria. There are steps that can and should be taken to reduce our vulnerability. And we can reduce the consequences if despite all of our efforts we "become infected," that is, the terrorists succeed, as on occasion they will.[4] Translated, this entails disruption (using intelligence, law enforcement, and military force), protection (homeland security, hardening buildings), and preparations to mitigate the consequences of inevitably successful actions (medical preparations, civil defense, and so on).

Success, then, cannot be defined in terms of eliminating or ending terrorism, any more than health can be defined as eliminating or ending all disease. We may eliminate a particular disease either by stamping out the cause (yellow fever) or by developing an effective vaccine (polio), but some diseases will prove resistant and new strains will emerge. The same holds for terrorism: We may destroy one group or capture and kill certain individuals, but terrorism in one or another form will persist.

We will not fail, as such. President George W. Bush made some political trouble for himself during the 2004 campaign when he suggested in an interview that it would be impossible to "win" the war on terror.[5] But the president was right on the merits if not the politics. Success in this context must be defined as reducing the ability of terrorists to cause destruction and enormous loss of life. The goal would be to reduce the level of international terrorism to its pre-9/11 impact, one that can better be described as a nuisance than as the principal threat to our society and way of life. (In this case, it was Senator Kerry who, using the word "nuisance," made political trouble for himself with this formulation. But he, too, was right on the merits if not the politics.[6]) For those who find this too modest or even defeatist, I would suggest it is anything but. The number of terrorists, the increased availability of technologies and materials that can cause mass destruction, the fundamental vulnerability of modern and relatively open societies such as the United States—all combine to make reducing terrorism to a nuisance level an ambitious undertaking and then some.

Not all terrorists are the same or can be dealt with by the same strategy. There are what might be described as "traditional" terrorists—the Irish Republican Army (IRA), the Basque separatists (ETA)—whose goals are specific and limited no matter how objectionable their tactics might be.

Limited goals can in principle be met through traditional diplomacy. The best approach in these cases is a mix of firmness (to attack them as one would any terrorist) and fairness (to meet those political objectives that are reasonable). Such an approach tends to lead to splits between relative moderates or pragmatists and those who are more radical and in the end can only be defeated.

All this stands in stark contrast to those who are better understood as "existential terrorists," namely, individuals and groups whose agendas are so far-reaching that they could never be satisfied through policy give-and-take or compromise. This applies to that brand of Islamic terrorist such as the al Qaeda adherent who seeks to avenge what he sees as history's wrongs and humiliations or who, for whatever reason, simply rejects the West. This terrorist, for whom terrorism is an end in itself or a means to ends so far-reaching that they could never realistically be met (a category that includes those Palestinian terrorists who reject a Jewish state), must be confronted.

There is an ongoing debate over whether those branded here as existential terrorists deserve the label. Are we hated for what we are or for what we do? Terrorists are not attacking the United States because of the Bill of Rights or because we enjoy freedom of speech or assembly. But some terrorists are seeking vengeance for perceived crimes and indignities visited upon Muslims by non-Muslims over the centuries or because they wish to establish Muslim ascendance throughout the world. The authors of the 9/11 Commission report argued that "Bin Ladin's grievance with the United States may have started in reaction to specific U.S. policies but it quickly became far deeper."[7]

"America is hated and attacked because Muslims believe they know precisely what the United States is doing in the Islamic world" is the conclusion of Michael Scheuer, author of the widely read book *Imperial Hubris*.[8] This perspective is echoed by the Defense Science Board, which in its September 2004 report to the Department of Defense argued that "Muslims do not 'hate our freedom,' but rather, they hate our policies. The overwhelming majority voice their objections to what they see as one-sided support in favor of Israel and against Palestinian rights, and the long-standing, even increasing support for what Muslims collectively see as tyrannies, most notably Egypt, Saudi Arabia, Jordan, Pakistan, and the Gulf states."[9]

A number of policies tend to be mentioned as most motivating to terrorists. The U.S. military presence in Afghanistan, Iraq, and Saudi Arabia is one. U.S. support for authoritarian and corrupt regimes in the region is another motivation in that there are Arabs and Muslims who resent what they see as their unworthy rulers, and who see terrorism as the best tool available to bring them down. This can translate into attacks on the United States, widely seen as the proverbial power behind the thrones. The United States is also criticized for supporting India in Kashmir, Russia in Chechnya, and China in Xinjiang—all viewed as anti-Muslim policies. For some reason, U.S. assistance to

Afghans against the Soviets, to Bosnians and Kosovars against Serbia, and to Kuwait against Iraq, as well as its support for Turkey's bid to join the EU, rarely if ever merits mention.

The Palestinian issue also figures prominently in this discussion of the causes of terrorism. I do not mean local Palestinian terror, which until now has largely focused on Israelis as targets. Such terror tends to be of two sorts: the more traditional, limited variety, which seeks to use terror to persuade Israelis to offer more at the negotiating table; and the more radical variety, which is looking not to influence Israeli diplomacy but rather to destroy Israel itself. Rather, most Arabs and Muslims around the world believe that the United States does not do enough to help Palestinians and does too much in support of Israel. There are individuals who believe that by attacking Americans they can lead the United States to reconsider its support for Israel or, failing that, at least achieve some degree of revenge or "justice" for what they see as American-facilitated Israeli attacks on Palestinians.

If this argument has merit, if it is correct to suggest that what motivates today's terrorists largely stems from U.S. behavior in the world, then the implication is clear: that terrorism against the United States and its partners would fall dramatically if the policies that allegedly led to terrorism were significantly altered. But although there is some limited truth to this claim—terrorists are motivated in part by what it is the United States does in the world—the disagreements of the terrorists with the United States and its partners are so profound that there is no way the United States could or should be willing to meet their objections through changes in its foreign policy.

The U.S. military presence in Saudi Arabia was and is resented, and this clearly is one of the original complaints of Osama bin Laden. But the U.S. presence in Saudi Arabia has never been an occupation. Although there was a large presence in 1990–1991 at the time of Operations Desert Shield and Desert Storm, it quickly declined to a few thousand in the years between the Gulf and Iraq wars. U.S. troops were an effective deterrent, preventing Saddam Hussein from invading the kingdom in the aftermath of his invasion and occupation of Kuwait. The U.S. presence in Saudi Arabia was also associated with operations mounted to implement UN resolutions protecting Iraqi citizens. The U.S. military presence in Saudi Arabia, which today only numbers in the hundreds, has always been relatively unobtrusive, as U.S. forces were and are mostly stationed in out-of-the-way locations far removed from Islamic holy places.

There were no U.S. forces in Afghanistan prior to 9/11. Forces were sent to defeat the Taliban. The country was never occupied. The bulk of the relatively modest U.S. military presence in Afghanistan (some 17,000 troops) is there to hunt down al Qaeda. NATO forces are in the country assisting the government, an effort that is both right and necessary. If all foreign forces were to suddenly leave, the relatively liberal Karzai government would almost certainly fall, to be replaced by the Taliban, bands of warlords, or some combination of the two.

Iraq is different. It has become a magnet and a school for terrorists. The presence of 150,000 U.S. soldiers attracts terrorists from around the world. The U.S. presence is also stimulating nationalist resistance from the Sunni minority in Iraq, resistance that is manifesting itself in the form of terrorism. All of this helps explain current and potential future terrorism, but not how we got to this point or any terrorism in the past.

Terrorism is aimed at weakening existing regimes. Saudi Arabia is a clear case in point. This is not for a moment to suggest that the current regime is attractive to us—in many ways far from it—or that we should accept it as it is. This is a rationale for the United States promoting reform, not withdrawing American support. Perspective is called for. Important U.S. interests (security cooperation, access to energy supplies, a willingness to accept Israel) are served by the policies of the current regime and would not be by any al Qaeda–supported successor. This is a lesson we should have learned from what took place in Iran twenty-five years ago, namely, that unattractive authoritarian regimes can be replaced by something far worse.

It is true that al Qaeda and like-minded terrorists derive some of their impetus from the Palestinian issue and from U.S. support for Israel. But this is not to suggest for a moment that Osama bin Laden did what he did on 9/11 because he wanted a Palestinian state or because he wanted the dividing line between a proposed Palestinian state and the state of Israel to be drawn differently. Osama bin Laden and those around him reject a two-state solution and want only one state, which happens not to be Israel. Clearly, this is unacceptable.

The Palestinian issue is one, however, that does contribute to the alienation and radicalism of *potential* terrorist recruits. There is a popular perception that the United States is anti-Arab and anti-Muslim and that U.S. foreign policy is filled with double standards that serve its interests but not theirs. Such perceptions make it much easier for terrorist groups to recruit new foot soldiers and more difficult for governments to work against them.

There is an important difference between existing terrorists and potential ones. Existing terrorists must be stopped. Preventing men and women from becoming terrorists in the first place is something quite different. U.S. policies can and do play a role here. This argues for minimizing the scale, visibility, and duration of U.S. military presence in the region, above all in Iraq. This is not to argue for an arbitrary withdrawal date being set; such exit dates are invariably counterproductive. But it is to argue for an exit strategy, one that conditions U.S. withdrawal on Iraqis (possibly helped by forces from Arab states as well as others) assuming an ever-increasing share of the security burden, something that requires accelerated training of Iraqi police and military personnel.

It also argues for actively promoting a Palestinian state.

The current situation in the Middle East serves the interests of no party to the dispute. Palestinians arguably pay the greatest price for the current situation. It is not just that they lack a state, but their standard of living is extremely low. Economic output has fallen, per capita GDP is under $1,000, and at least one-third of the labor force is unemployed. They face the daily humiliation of occupation. Violence is a regular feature of life. If Palestine existed as a separate state, it would be considered failing or failed.

But Israel also pays a substantial price for the status quo. As Americans are learning to their dismay in Iraq, being an occupier is costly in every sense. Israel also suffers the physical, economic, and psychological costs of terrorist attacks. There are as well the demographic and political stakes, in that Israel cannot endure as a democratic and Jewish state and also remain in control of a large and fast-growing Palestinian population.

The price the United States pays for the current state of affairs may be less obvious, but it is no less real. The perception in the Arab and Muslim worlds (and in Europe for that matter) that U.S. support empowers Israel is a principal source of anti-Americanism. This perception makes it more difficult for local governments to be seen working with the United States. It also makes it more difficult for the United States to be an effective proponent of reform in the region, as the messenger is neither trusted nor welcome.

The willingness of the George W. Bush administration

to publicly call for the creation of an independent state of Palestine was thus an important development, one with the potential to make a big difference in diplomatic prospects and in perceptions of the United States. Where the administration came up short was in not doing enough to promote it. It was and is not enough to say the United States stands by the "road map" (the document put forward by the United States, Russia, the EU, and the UN in 2003 to guide Middle East peace efforts) if at the same time the United States fails to make it a diplomatic priority. Nor does it help to speak publicly, as the United States did in April 2004, of those aspects of final status welcomed by Israelis—Palestinians should have the right to return only to Palestine, Israel should be able to hold on to territory that reflects certain post-1967 demographic changes—without speaking of other final status issues likely to appeal to Palestinians. In order to give Palestinians incentive to act responsibly, the United States needs to make clear its support for a territorial division based on the 1967 lines, with territorial compensation to the Palestinians for the limited land outside those lines that Israel does end up keeping. The United States also hurt itself by not doing much more to rein in Israeli settlement and construction activity that is in many instances inconsistent with trying to bring about a viable Palestinian state.

The death of longtime Palestinian leader Yasser Arafat in November 2004 is an important development, potentially a turning point. It allowed for a new and legitimate

Palestinian leadership to emerge through elections, a leadership that appears prepared to disavow terrorism and to do a good deal to stop those who are still wedded to using force to attack Israel and Israelis. Israeli prime minister Ariel Sharon's plan to disengage (withdraw) unilaterally from occupied Gaza as well as from selected areas of the northern West Bank and to dismantle several Israeli settlements in the process is another important development. So, too, is the formation in early 2005 of a new Israeli government with broader and more centrist political support. The February 2005 cease-fire accord is evidence of the changed situation. There is an opportunity to make major strides toward a solution of this long-festering conflict, but only if the United States actively solicits the help of others, including the EU, Japan, Russia, the UN, and Arab states such as Egypt, in working with the Palestinians to develop the capacities of a modern state, in making sure that Israeli withdrawals do not create security vacuums filled by terrorists, and in promoting negotiations that address the core issues of the conflict.

There are, of course, obstacles to realizing this opportunity. One is continued terrorism from Palestinian groups such as Hamas. Another is substantial opposition within Israel to meaningful territorial compromise. A third is a new emphasis on democracy, and in particular Palestinian democracy, as a prerequisite for peace. "Israel must link its concessions to the degree of openness, transparency, and liberalization of its neighbors."[10] This is what is advocated by Natan Sharansky (the former Soviet dissident who is now a member of Israel's parliament) and supported at least to some degree by President Bush.[11] A democratic Palestine is certainly desirable, but it should not be viewed as essential. Requiring that Palestine be democratic would put off any peace negotiation for years, which would only fuel radicalism and violence. History also shows that democracy is not essential for avoiding war. Israel has had peaceful relations with nondemocratic Egypt and Jordan for decades, and the United States, which avoided war with the Soviet Union for most of the twentieth century, now has often cooperative ties with China and Russia, neither of which can be described as democratic. What should matter most is not the character of the future government of Palestine so much as its willingness and ability to sign a peace treaty with Israel and live up to its obligations.

American foreign policy must deal with the societies producing young men and women terrorists. It is correct to point out that 99 percent or more of Arabs and Muslims worldwide are not terrorists, but it is no less correct to point out that the bulk of today's terrorists around the world are in fact Arabs and Muslims. Moreover, Islamic terrorism poses a threat of a different order of magnitude. As the authors of the 9/11 Commission report noted, "[T]he enemy is not just 'terrorism,' some generic evil. . . . The catastrophic threat at this moment in history is more specific. It is the threat posed by Islamist terrorism—especially the al Qaeda network, its affiliates, and its ideology."[12] Doing something about this requires not simply considering what can be done to reduce the motives of the terrorists but also what can be done to reduce their readiness to be recruited in the first place. Interestingly, the problem does not seem to be poverty per se, which may be a contributing cause of civil wars but not terror. A good many of those involved in the 9/11 attacks were anything but poor. Also, most of those young men and women who are in fact poor, be they in Arab countries or anywhere else, do not become terrorists.

Arab societies are for the most part characterized by sclerotic, top-heavy political systems that offer little possibility for citizens to determine their own fates. Elections are rare and, when they do occur, often put into place individuals with little real power. Independent organizations are difficult to establish; those that can be established often lack real independence. In many societies, the mosque (as the one institution many governments are reluctant to crack down on) has been the principal gathering point for those unhappy with some aspect of government policy. Not surprisingly, this gives religious activists disproportionate attention and influence.

These political limits are reinforced by economic and educational limitations. Many Arab countries are plagued by too much government ownership, widespread corruption, and a regulatory environment that discourages foreign investment. Even Saudi Arabia, blessed with large pools of oil and gas, is little better off, as the bulk of the population is not employed in meaningful jobs. To some extent these pervasive problems are the direct result of education systems that emphasize rote memorization of texts over encouraging inquiry and do little to equip young men, and even less young women, with the tools they need to function well in a competitive global economy.[13]

The net effect is societies with large numbers of disaffected, underemployed young people who are often drawn to the rhetoric of fundamental religion and radical politics. Doing something about this, promoting significant change in the societies and economies in the Muslim and particularly Arab worlds, needs to be a foreign policy priority. The requirement for change is great. This translates into helping governments reform their education systems by introducing modern curricula and teaching methods. On the economic side, it means encouraging governments to create conditions demonstrated worldwide to support private sector activity. Politically, it argues for advocating and supporting the development of civil society and accountable government. We need to foster a clash within a civilization if we are to avoid a clash between civilizations.

Promoting reform from the outside must always be handled with sensitivity and perspective.[14] There are important "do's" and "don'ts" alike. Neither the United States nor anyone else should insist on any single or particular model of democracy or market. Anything that succeeds must take root in local societies and traditions. Promoting reform is something outsiders must do *with* local governments, organizations, and people, not *to* them. This is critical, because the United States has to maintain good working relations with the same leaders and governments it seeks to change. Reform will not come overnight, and we should not require that it do so. The time horizon is more likely to be decades than years. Women must be included; no society can flourish that denies itself the talents of half its people. Access of girls to education and of women to resources to start businesses has been shown to be critical to the prospects of entire societies.[15]

Political and economic reform tend to be mutually reinforcing in that the elements required in a modern economy—the rule of law, transparency, room for individual initiative—are exactly the same things that a modern democracy requires. The same can be said for education reform and its ties to political and economic change: An informed and skilled populace is essential for both a working democracy and economic success. But introducing political and economic change in tandem can at times prove impossible, largely because of the government. When this is the case, emphasizing economic measures early on makes the most sense. Often, such changes are accepted by regimes that understand the need for improved economic performance yet resist political reform for fear of relinquishing power. Over time, however, economic reform is likely to help the emergence of a middle class, historically often associated with demands for political change.

One aspect of political reform, that of elections, merits special attention. Too often many observers equate democracy and elections. One does not guarantee the other. What makes a country truly democratic is that power is distributed—within the government, so that no individual can rule without constraint, and between government and society, so that government cannot dictate all that goes on. It is important that the judiciary, the legislature, the media, political parties, corporations, unions, and civic groups enjoy true independence. Such constitutional checks and balances are essential. To have elections without such controls means that the election itself is likely to be flawed and that whoever wins will have too much power concentrated in his or her hands. "One man, one vote, one time" is something to be avoided. The United States has nothing to fear from elections, even elections that result in the coming to power of some anti-American party or person, so long as that power is limited and an opposition will have a fair chance of replacing it one day. As a rule, "electocracy" should not be confused with democracy.

The United States can do much to assist and promote reform efforts. Public statements and private advice can create support for change and help launch debates. Economic resources can empower civil society. Exchanges that bring students and young professionals to the United States can introduce new ideas and provide valuable experience. Teacher and language training, translation of texts, the adoption of modern curricula—all can improve the quality of education. Radios, television, and the Internet can be used to broadcast messages and information that otherwise would not reach people who, in the absence of such material, are dependent on official sources of information and the mosque.[16]

There is reason to believe that we are making progress. A number of factors—the example of Ukraine's "Orange Revolution," images of Afghans, Palestinians, and Iraqis voting freely, the reaction in Lebanon to the assassination of a former prime minister, growing intellectual ferment within the Arab world, and George W. Bush's strong rhetoric—all have had positive impact. Political, economic, and social change is finally coming to the Middle East. The challenge now is to make sure this process spreads and takes root in all Arab countries, including Egypt (the region's most populous) and Saudi Arabia (its wealthiest).

Where, then, do we stand in the struggle against terrorism? Secretary of Defense Donald Rumsfeld admitted that he did not know: "Today, we lack the metrics to know if we are winning or losing the global war on terror. Are we capturing, killing, or deterring and dissuading more terrorists every day than the madrassas and the radical clerics are recruiting, training, and deploying against us?"[17]

There are no statistics that enable anyone to answer Secretary Rumsfeld's question with certainty. But we can say that the world is more integrated than ever before in the struggle against existing terrorists. There is little or no tolerance for terrorism, and improved intelligence, law enforcement, and homeland security have made not just the United States but others less vulnerable. The potential to make inroads against terrorist recruitment also exists. Prospects are better than at any time in years for significant progress on the Israel-Palestinian conflict. Prospects for reforming Arab societies that have become breeding grounds for terrorists are also better than at any time in history. The matter of reform is now squarely on the U.S. and European foreign policy agendas, and there is a growing debate within the Arab world itself about the need for political, economic, educational, and social change. The opportunity to realize major gains in what promises to be a decades-long struggle against modern day terror is at hand.

4

•

Nukes on the Loose

THE WORLD would be a much safer place if states accepted that they have the responsibility not to facilitate in any way the spread or proliferation of weapons of mass destruction in general and nuclear weapons in particular. Ideally, states would commit to do everything in their power to frustrate the proliferation of all weapons of mass destruction and modern delivery systems such as ballistic missiles.

This sounds obvious: fewer nuclear weapons, safer world. But there is a widely held view that avers that the principal reason the Cold War never went hot (unlike, say, the other two great struggles of the twentieth century) was because leaders of both the United States and the Soviet Union concluded that the costs of nuclear war were so great that no cause justified fighting one. In principle, the argument goes, such a balance (and the resulting state of mutual deterrence) could be re-created in other settings, in the process reducing the chance of conflict of any sort, given that the possible escalation to nuclear exchange might introduce a note of caution into the behavior of the protagonists.[1]

There are several problems with this view. First, although nuclear weapons did add a dimension of stability to U.S.-Soviet relations, they did so only after many years and after both the United States and the Soviet Union in the 1960s developed the capacity to retaliate so robustly that they reduced dramatically the advantage that would accrue to the side that struck first. Getting to that point is easier said than done. One or another government today might be tempted to strike before some other country it viewed as an adversary reached the point of assured retaliation. This would constitute a classic case of preventive war.

It would be even harder to ensure stability if there were a larger number of nuclear weapons states, something that could easily become a reality in the Middle East if Iran were to develop nuclear weapons and such countries as Saudi Arabia, Syria, and Egypt followed suit. Mutually assured destruction is a simple concept ill-suited to a complex multipolar region or world. Managing relations and maintaining order amid a half-dozen nuclear states that are hostile or at least suspicious toward one another is an extraordinarily difficult challenge. There is the chance of accidental or unauthorized launch or mistaken intelligence suggesting a launch when in fact none has occurred; the United States and the Soviet Union had a number of close calls, and no one should assume that others will be as fortunate. Perhaps most important, there is the danger that nuclear weapons could fall into the wrong hands because of theft by terrorists or others owing to a lack of adequate security (the concern about Russia), because of the disintegration of governmental authority (the concern in Pakistan), or because a government determines to make technology, materials, or weapons available for reasons of ideology, profit, or both. The impact of the private network run out of Pakistan that contributed to the nuclear efforts of such countries as North Korea and Libya makes this painfully clear.[2]

As of now, the nuclear club consists of at least eight, and possibly nine, countries. In addition to the original five states "permitted" to have nuclear weapons under the 1970 Treaty on the Non-Proliferation of Nuclear Weapons (NPT)—the United States, Russia, Great Britain, France, and China—the list of nuclear weapons states now includes Israel, India, Pakistan (three countries not party to the NPT), and perhaps North Korea. Moreover, even that number could increase and come to include additional states as well as actors other than states, such as al Qaeda. The idea has gained ground that nuclear weapons are a source of status, a way to get a seat at the table and to be taken seriously. They are also seen as a way to deter the United States from invading or to inflict great damage on the United States; the fact that nonnuclear Iraq was attacked twice in just over a decade and North Korea, almost certainly nuclear, has thus far escaped attack, has not gone unnoticed.

So we have arrived at a critical historical juncture, described by one recent study as a tipping point: "Should current proliferation trends continue, within the next decade there may be more declared nuclear weapons states, more undeclared nuclear weapons states, and more states developing nuclear weapons than ever before."[3] Either the international community will succeed in stopping the spread of nuclear weapons, or we could soon find ourselves in a world of twelve or fifteen or even more nuclear weapons states. Ideally, an international consensus would form around steps that could be taken to cap or, better yet, roll back the North Korean and Iranian programs. In addition, governments would agree to shore up global arrangements designed to see that no state or terrorist organization develops or acquires either nuclear weapons or the nuclear fuel (either enriched uranium or plutonium) that is the critical but difficult-to-produce element of a nuclear weapon.

The architecture—or at least the plans—for integration already exist. The Nuclear Non-Proliferation Treaty certifies that only five countries—the United States, Russia, China, Britain, and France—are legitimate "Nuclear Weapons States." These five states commit not to transfer nuclear weapons and not to provide fissile material or equipment needed to produce such material to anyone else unless it is placed under controls (safeguards) operated by the International Atomic Energy Agency (IAEA). The NPT also commits the five to make technology available so long as it is used for peaceful purposes and to reduce and ultimately eliminate their own stockpiles of nuclear weapons. All other (non–nuclear weapons) states that sign the treaty commit to not receiving or developing nuclear weapons or information that would help them manufacture such weapons.

There are many other agreements, including bans on nuclear testing and various supplier groups created to keep critical materials, technologies, and delivery systems out of the wrong hands, be they states of proliferation concern or nonstate actors.[4] These supplier groups are now complemented by the Proliferation Security Initiative (PSI), an undertaking launched in 2003 by the United States and ten other countries (the number has since grown to more than sixty) that agree to share intelligence and coordinate diplomatically, legally, and militarily in an effort to interdict shipments of unauthorized nuclear-related material, regardless of how they are being transported.[5] This exchange of intelligence in October 2003 led to the detention of a German-owned vessel (the BBC *China*) carrying centrifuges to Libya.

There are international agreements banning the possession of both chemical and biological weapons. UN Security Council Resolution 1540 (passed in April 2004) calls on states to put into place domestic controls to minimize the chance that any technology or material related to nuclear or other weapons of mass destruction could get into the hands of any terrorist group. The G-8 gathering of major industrialized countries meeting in Sea Island, Georgia, in June 2004 agreed to dedicate substantial resources (up to $20 billion by 2012) to making sure nuclear material in Russia and elsewhere is rendered harmless and that scientists with specialized knowledge are retrained so they need not sell their expertise to some terrorist group or government with nuclear ambitions.

But all these agreements are not enough. The NPT itself is seriously flawed. There is no requirement that countries join it, and no penalty if they decide to leave. Only three months' notice is required of countries wishing to withdraw. Under the guise of maintaining a nuclear power (electricity-generating) program, a country can develop or acquire much of the technology and fissile material it needs to build nuclear weapons and still remain within the treaty's provisions; by the time it "breaks out," it is too late to prevent it from becoming a nuclear weapons state. (This is potentially the situation with Iran.) Cheating is not all that difficult, and the world's nuclear monitoring body, the IAEA, traditionally has only had the right to inspect those facilities declared (and made available to IAEA inspectors) by member governments.

Several reforms are needed. No country should be allowed to import equipment or technology that would give it access to either highly enriched uranium or plutonium, the explosive material of a nuclear bomb; those who need nuclear fuel for reasons of electricity generation should be able to receive it at a reasonable or even subsidized price, but only if the fuel remains under adequate international control such as that provided by the IAEA. Also needed is agreement that countries that deny IAEA inspectors access to suspected but undeclared nuclear sites (something called for by the "Additional Protocol") should be denied any technology or equipment that could support a nuclear program of any sort, as should any country that withdraws from the NPT.[6]

Virtually all of these proposals were made by President Bush in his February 11, 2004, speech at the National Defense University.[7] The proposals were then discussed by the G-8 countries when they met four months later in Georgia. Many of the U.S. ideas were reflected at least in part in the G-8 document dealing with these issues, which among other things stated collective support for the Additional Protocol and agreement on a one-year moratorium "not to inaugurate new initiatives involving transfer of enrichment and reprocessing equipment and technologies to additional states."[8] Just weeks before the G-8 meeting, the French government circulated a proposal that would require would-be recipients of sensitive enrichment-related technologies and equipment to demonstrate a credible need for nuclear power and accept the Additional Protocol. The French proposal also called for stronger supplier arrangements and called on all states to suspend nuclear cooperation with any country for which the IAEA cannot provide assurances that their nuclear program is devoted exclusively to peaceful purposes.[9]

None of this deals directly with three nuclear weapons countries—Israel, India, and Pakistan—that never joined the NPT. On one level, there is not much to be done about any of them: None is about to give up its nuclear weapons.

Israel views its weapons as the ultimate guarantor of its existence, given that it still confronts a far more populous and largely hostile Arab world. The only realistic prospect for dealing with Israel's nuclear arsenal is in the context of a comprehensive regional peace that leaves Israel feeling welcome and secure; alas, this is not going to happen any time soon. India wants its nuclear weapons to counter its nuclear neighbors, China and Pakistan, and because it rejects the notion that some powers merit nuclear weapons status, but not India. Pakistan's motives are mostly tied to India's, which rules out rolling back what now exists.

There is no avoiding the double standards that are built into the nuclear nonproliferation regime. The best thing that can be done is to treat these three states as de facto members of the club and to work with them so that they do nothing that contributes to additional proliferation. This applies most to Pakistan, a country with a record that does not inspire confidence, given that it was host to the activities of A. Q. Khan, the man who "privatized" the spread of nuclear technology around the world. An integrated foreign policy requires the United States to work with these countries to reduce the possibility that nuclear weapons will ever be used, be it intentionally as an act of war or because of accident or unauthorized command. Gaining international agreement on all of the above is not as difficult as it may sound, in part because it essentially boils down to accepting reality and avoiding difficult choices. The problem of double standards exists more with reference to other medium-sized countries (such as Brazil) that resent the discrimination and uneven application of international rules.

Another accusation of double standards, however, can be rebutted. The United States preaches and devotes itself to the cause of nuclear nonproliferation while maintaining a sizable nuclear weapons arsenal of its own. This seems hypocritical, but it is not. Even if the other major powers declared their willingness to eliminate their nuclear weapons, verifying the promises would likely be impossible. What is more, as reductions progressed, it would introduce a greater likelihood of instability as it raised the incentive to cheat: Suddenly a relatively modest arsenal could be militarily and politically meaningful. A parallel example offers a more likely scenario: The United States no longer maintains any chemical or biological weapons yet they have become the despots' WMD of choice. It is also worth noting that the greatest challenges to nonproliferation efforts have occurred over the last decade, precisely at a time when U.S. inventories were reduced to levels considerably lower than their Cold War highs.

The United States should do all that it can to reduce the currency and symbolic value of nuclear weapons and to delegitimize their possession and use. Accelerating implementation of the May 2002 Moscow Treaty on Strategic Offensive Reductions, in which the United States and Russia agreed to reduce their strategic nuclear warheads by approximately two-thirds (down to a level of 1,700–2,200) by the end of 2012, would be a positive gesture. It would also make sense to revise the agreement so that neither party would be allowed to keep as spares or store any warheads taken out of "operationally deployed" status. Consistent with this, the United States should reconsider its interest in developing a new generation of nuclear weapons. It is not clear they are necessary—highly accurate and powerful conventional munitions can accomplish the same tasks (such as destroying underground nuclear laboratories or facilities elsewhere) if the intelligence is available—and nuclear warheads will not help if accurate intelligence does not exist. The use of "miniature" nuclear weapons would work to weaken the taboo against nuclear weapons that has grown up and strengthened over the past sixty years. Going ahead with new nuclear weapons production will make it much harder for the United States to argue effectively in public and in private that others should forgo such weapons. Similarly, U.S. opposition to such arms control proposals as a comprehensive test ban and a ban on producing fissile material needs to be reconsidered; it is not clear the strategic benefits outweigh the costs of diluting U.S. efforts to persuade others not to develop nuclear weapons.

The United States also ought to consider adopting a new declaratory policy, one of "no first use" of nuclear weapons or any unconventional weapon of mass destruction. During the Cold War, the United States rejected adopting a policy of "no first use," largely because it and NATO relied on nuclear weapons and possible use of them to deter a Soviet–Warsaw

Pact invasion of Western Europe and in case deterrence failed to compensate for what was thought to be a large Soviet–Warsaw Pact conventional military advantage. None of this applies now. It is the United States that enjoys conventional military superiority and its relations with other major powers are such that nuclear first use is out of the question. It is difficult to imagine why the United States would need to resort to first use of nuclear weapons; far more likely is that it wants to do everything possible to discourage others from using them first. Declaratory policies do not alter capabilities or potential actions; still, adopting such a verbal posture would further delegitimize the acquisition and use of nuclear weapons by others.

The Hard Cases: North Korea and Iran

As is OFTEN the case, international consensus tends to come under strain when it comes down to specific cases and specific remedies. The two most salient are North Korea and Iran. Why North Korea wants a nuclear weapons capability or at least option is a matter of conjecture. Plausible explanations include deterrence of a possible U.S. attack, as leverage (to be traded away) in a negotiation, or as something to be sold for much-needed cash. None of these arguments needs be mutually exclusive.[10]

There is no enthusiasm outside Pyongyang for a North Korean nuclear capability. China worries for good reason that it could lead Japan and South Korea (or, one day, a unified Korea) to follow suit. China also sees no advantage in a war that for a second time (the first being the Korean War more than a half century ago) would bring American forces into North Korea near the Chinese border. Japan worries for its own security. The United States may worry the most of all, fearing not only the consequences of a North Korean nuclear arsenal for the region but also for the world, given North Korea's economic weakness and the possibility it may see nuclear weapons as something to be sold for hard currency—a concern reinforced by its history of counterfeiting, selling drugs as well as missile technology and parts, and its participation in the A. Q. Khan proliferation network.

The question is how best to ensure that a North Korean nuclear arsenal does not come about. China's role is central: It has more (although still limited) influence with North Korea than anyone else. China is the source of much of North Korea's energy and is its principal trading partner. But China, while willing to apply some pressure, seems reluctant to insist out of fear that if North Korea began to collapse, there could be war on the peninsula and massive refugee flows into China. Some Chinese leaders may also want to avoid appearing disloyal to a fellow Communist country that it has supported in one way or another for its entire existence. As a result, China's objective appears to be more one of placing a ceiling on the problem than of actually resolving it.

It may be too late in any event. North Korea announced in February 2005 that it possesses nuclear weapons. Most experts believe that North Korea either possesses several nuclear bombs or at least the material to fuel six to ten of them. There are a limited number of options at this point for the United States and others to pursue. One is to accept a new, de facto status for North Korea, akin to what has become the U.S. and international approach to Israel, India, and Pakistan. Given North Korea's history, though, there would need to be a much greater threat attached to its using a nuclear weapon or transferring critical technologies, fuel, or weapons to others, be they states or terrorist groups. The United States should declare publicly that any government that uses, threatens to use, or knowingly transfers weapons of mass destruction or key materials to third parties opens itself up to the strongest sanctions, not to exclude attack and removal from power. This should be accompanied by a concerted diplomatic effort to get the other major powers to sign on to such a statement. Consensus among the major powers would send a strong deterrent signal and possibly increase support for (or at least decrease opposition to) U.S.-led military action if deterrence were to fail and nuclear weapons were in fact used or transferred by a country such as North Korea.

The risk inherent in an approach that accepts a North Korean nuclear arsenal is that North Korea is a desperate failing country led by a regime that might do anything to stay in power. There is also the danger that the North might transfer nuclear material to some terrorist group in exchange for much-needed money, believing it could do so without the knowledge of the United States. In short, deterrence might not work.

A second option is to turn to diplomacy. In principle, the North, arguably the least integrated country in the world, might receive a number of benefits, including economic assistance, security assurances, and political standing, if it satisfied U.S. and international concerns regarding its nuclear program. But it is far from clear that such an agreement could be negotiated—and, even if it could, that it would be implemented faithfully. North Korea violated its 1990 accord with South Korea to keep the peninsula free of nuclear weapons, and it acted inconsistently with the spirit of the 1994 U.S.-North Korean Agreed Framework, an agreement in which North Korea committed itself to not reprocessing nuclear fuel and to cooperating fully with the International Atomic Energy Agency, when it initiated a clandestine program to enrich uranium.[11]

Despite these problems, diplomacy must be pursued— in part because it could succeed, in part because only by making a good faith effort and failing is there any chance the United States could garner the requisite regional and international backing for a more confrontational tack, one that would begin with sanctions and conceivably escalate to the use of military force. Better yet would be to approach diplomacy and the credible threat of force not so much as alternatives to be tried in sequence but as complements; indeed, there is a strong argument that the diplomatic track has a chance of succeeding only if it is tightly coupled with a credible threat of severe penalties (including the use of military force) should North Korea not do what the international community demands of it.

There are dangers in pursuing this second course. North Korea might exploit the time any negotiation requires to enhance its capabilities. It could of course simply cheat after it signs an agreement. Even absent such bad faith, rewarding a country such as North Korea with alternative energy sources and various political and economic accords for its nuclear "investment" could have the perverse effect of feeding proliferation elsewhere by encouraging other countries to follow suit in the belief that they, too, will be "rewarded" for bad behavior. There are no perfect policies available at this point. One must always weigh the costs of any alternatives, in this case those associated with either tolerating a North Korean nuclear arsenal or going to war.

A third option involves the use of military force. The degree of potential international acceptance of (or resistance to) this option will depend on circumstances. There is, for example, considerable international support in principle for the right of anticipatory self-defense. This idea is not particularly new; it was Franklin Roosevelt who in a fireside chat in September 1941 told the American people that "when you see a rattlesnake poised to strike, you do not wait until he has struck before you crush him. . . ."[12] This is akin to what Israel did in 1967 upon receipt of tactical warning of an imminent Egyptian attack. But what is critical here is that the intelligence assessment of the threat be near 100-percent accurate, confirming that the danger is in fact imminent and that there is no other available means to stop it. Under such rare circumstances, it is widely viewed that a state enjoys a right to preempt, to strike before it is certain to be struck. This is preemption in the classical sense, something quite different from George W. Bush's use of the term, which in fact is better understood as prevention. The "problem" for policymakers is that North Korea is unlikely to ever satisfy the conditions that would warrant a preemptive strike in the traditional sense.

Far more likely are situations in which the available intelligence is questionable, the threat uncertain but in no way clearly imminent, and the military option but one of several policies available. Such situations raise the possibility of preventive attacks. There is no international consensus of any sort as regards prevention, which involves the use of force against a gathering but not imminent threat. The Israeli strike on the Osirak nuclear complex in 1981 is one example of prevention, as is the attack by the U.S.-led coalition on Iraq some two decades later. Although the Bush administration described its strategy as "preemption," the substance of its position toward Iraq constituted a clear case of "prevention," given the uncertain knowledge of Iraqi capabilities and the complete lack of evidence of any imminence of hostile attack by Iraq.

The reason for the controversy surrounding preventive

attacks is that more than any other potential form of military intervention, they threaten to undermine (and not just dilute) the international conventions governing state sovereignty and proscribing unprovoked interventions involving military force. Prevention can easily be cited as a justification for acting militarily by those looking for a pretext. A world in which preventive attacks were common would be a dangerous and disorderly world, in some ways an undesirable throwback to times in which states regularly involved themselves in the internal affairs of their neighbors.

It is in part for this reason (as well as the possibility of retaliation) that a bias has grown up against preventive attacks. The United States eschewed preventive strikes against the Soviet Union in the early years of the Cold War and discouraged the Soviet Union from carrying out preventive military action against China when the Sino-Soviet dispute intensified in the late 1960s and early 1970s. The Reagan administration was quite critical of Israel's preventive strike against Iraq two decades ago, while more recently, the United States discouraged India from preventive attacks on its neighbor Pakistan.

The question today is whether we have the luxury of continuing to oppose preventive action, given the proliferation of weapons of mass destruction. As is obvious, the Bush administration decided (at least in the Iraq case) that we do not. Its reasoning was straightforward: Retaliation is not a viable strategy when an initial strike by an adversary armed with nuclear weapons could cause enormous loss of life and great destruction. Moreover, the secrecy that increasingly characterizes such capabilities and programs makes waiting for clear warning of potential use (in order to meet the "imminence" threshold required for preemptive strikes) unrealistic.[13]

When the Bush administration decided to press the case for prevention against Iraq, it did not persuade many governments or people outside the United States as to the legitimacy of the U.S.-led intervention. The failure to uncover weapons of mass destruction in Iraq will inevitably cast suspicion on future U.S. allegations of the sort and make future preventive actions more difficult for the United States or anyone else to undertake with any degree of international support. So, too, will the reality that the war's aftermath has gone less well than many forecast.

Iraq aside, other governments are sure to argue that a preventive strike against alleged weapons of mass destruction lacks legitimacy because the United States is inconsistent in its position (it has not preventively attacked Israel, India, or Pakistan) or because there are other policy tools (most notably diplomacy) available. The apparent success in persuading Libya to give up its nuclear program will reinforce the argument against the necessity to intervene forcefully.[14] Preventive strikes are quite difficult to carry out successfully, given the secrecy surrounding nuclear programs; the resulting intelligence requirements can be insurmountable. For example, it is not at all clear what North Korea has or where it has it. In such cases, there would be the option to strike at targets valued by the government in order to coerce it into meeting U.S. and international demands regarding its nuclear programs. It is not clear, though, that such strikes could be sustained politically or that they would have the desired effect. The outcome of all this is that other governments will resist viewing preventive attacks as legitimate unless they are backed by a UN or some other broad international mandate and then only after other policies have been shown to have been tried and to have failed. Even this may not be enough in the case of North Korea, where its neighbors (most importantly South Korea, but also Japan, China, and Russia) are likely to oppose any preventive strikes out of fear it would lead to a war on the Korean Peninsula that could well leave hundreds of thousands dead and the economy of South Korea and the region (and possibly beyond) devastated.

The only sure way to denuclearize North Korea would be to invade it, take control of the entire country, and remove the regime. The expense of carrying out a preventive war along the lines of what was done in Iraq (as opposed to more limited preventive strikes) would be enormous. North Korea's conventional military power could cause great loss of life and physical destruction in the South; use of nuclear weapons would obviously increase such costs by an order of magnitude. Many U.S. military personnel (including the 30,000 currently stationed in South Korea, along with reinforcements sure to be sent) would lose their lives. Such a war would cause great regional and global economic upheaval. It is a war that could and would be won, but only at great cost.

What, then, should the United States do about North Korea? U.S. policy during the first term of George W. Bush's presidency was a diluted hybrid of the first two non-military options described above. On the one hand, North Korea developed several nuclear weapons (or at least enough fissile material for them) without paying any clear price. There is thus a reality of de facto acceptance of what North Korea has done, despite U.S. rhetoric to the contrary. On the other hand, the United States (working with China, Japan, Russia, and South Korea) at the same time initiated a series of discussions with North Korea about what it expected from it in the nonproliferation realm and what it could expect in return. The package of incentives finally put forward in 2004 fell short of what the North would accept, while the failure to include any clear penalties for refusing to cooperate meant that North Korea was under little pressure to compromise. Neither the carrot nor the stick was adequate. Valuable time was lost in resisting a bilateral U.S.–North Korean negotiation. It matters little whether China, Japan, South Korea, and Russia are physically in the room so long as the United States coordinates its policies with them.

It does little good to say that the United States and the world never should have allowed matters to reach this point. The best—or, more accurately, least bad—path available now would be to continue to work with South Korea,

Japan, China, and Russia on a diplomatic package through which the North would receive security assurances, energy assistance, and specified political and economic benefits in exchange for giving up its nuclear programs (fuel and weapons alike) and agreeing to international inspections that provided considerable confidence that it had kept its word. The five countries would also need to agree on economic and political sanctions to be imposed on the North if it failed to accept such an agreement by a specified date or if it crossed some "red line" such as testing a nuclear device.

The United States should not rule out the use of military force against known North Korean nuclear-related sites. The danger, of course, is that the United States would not be able to target and destroy all the relevant sites and that by attacking, it could trigger retaliation by the North against South Korea. The leaders of the North would need to understand that any retaliation of any sort would lead to a war that would end with regime change, that is, their removal from power, and the effective end to North Korea as a separate state. U.S. foreign policy must press the governments of South Korea and Japan not to rule out such a scenario. Nor can the United States tolerate any North Korean transfer or use of nuclear material.

It is not clear the United States could persuade any other country to support using military force against the North; it is also doubtful it has the capacity to fight a war in North Korea at this time, given U.S. involvements elsewhere, most notably in Iraq. But simply raising the prospect of force should boost diplomatic prospects so long as a credible diplomatic offer is also tabled. What matters is not whether China supports the policy so much as that it motivates China to use all of its influence to persuade North Korea to agree to eschew a nuclear weapons program. To this end, the U.S. government must reassure China's leaders as to long-term U.S. thinking regarding Northeast Asia: that the United States is firmly opposed to the emergence of any new nuclear weapons state in the region, a posture that covers both Japan and a unified Korea. It may be more difficult to persuade South Korea (which would bear the brunt of any war) to support a robust option, but the United States cannot be expected to support a policy of avoiding a war no matter what, lest it forfeit the most important source of leverage vis-à-vis North Korea.

Iran

IRAN'S NUCLEAR program raises many of the same issues. The program is of long standing; its roots go back to the time of the shah. Iran's interest in developing nuclear weapons (or at least developing the option) is opaque, but it seems to reflect some mix of prestige, deterrence of the United States, and strategic assessment, given the dangerous neighborhood in which it finds itself.[15]

Iran's nuclear program is more developed than many believed was the case. In August 2002, the world learned that

Iran had created part of the centrifuge capacity it would need to enrich uranium, a process that involves first converting uranium into a gas and then using special centrifuges to increase the concentration of the Uranium-235 isotope. (A low concentration of U-235 is best for power generation, a high concentration for weapons.) Although enrichment for power-generation purposes is allowed under the Non-Proliferation Treaty, Iran never met the obligation of treaty members to inform the IAEA of what it was doing. This naturally set off alarm bells around the world. In 2003, the governments of France, Germany, and the United Kingdom (anxious to head off a confrontation between Iran and the United States) persuaded Iran to suspend its enrichment program in exchange for assurances that certain nuclear-related technologies and fuel would be transferred to Iran. They also agreed to block the United States from raising the issue in the UN Security Council, something that could have resulted in sanctions against Iran. Iran did submit to a number of IAEA inspections designed to clear up questions as to what exactly it was doing. But Iran then announced in the summer of 2004 that it would resume production and assembly of centrifuges central to enriching uranium. Adding to the concern is the fact that Iran also announced its plans to start producing uranium gas (another step in the enrichment chain) and that it was developing several other facilities that could be used to develop explosive material for nuclear weapons. Subsequent efforts by the three European governments and the

IAEA did not resolve the question of either Iran's capabilities or intentions.[16]

It strains credulity that Iran, a country blessed with enormous natural gas reserves and the second-largest pool of proven oil reserves in the world, has a real need for nuclear power to generate electricity. There is also good reason for concern stemming from Iran's pattern of deception relating to its nuclear program, its support for terrorism, and its development of medium-range missiles. Clearly, the U.S. and many other governments believe that Iran ought not to be allowed to realize any ambitions it may harbor when it comes to developing nuclear weapons. The question is the extent to which the major powers are prepared to jeopardize their relationship with and interests in Iran (not to mention the costs they are prepared to bear) for the sake of this objective.

Using military force—preventive strikes—to destroy Iran's developing program is easier said than done, given imperfect intelligence about what Iran has and where it has it and the operational military challenges of attacking distant and buried facilities. It is possible, however, that such strikes might succeed in destroying some of Iran's facilities in part or in whole and thereby set back its program by a matter of months or even years. Even if this were to occur, Iran would surely reconstitute its program in a manner that would make future strikes even more difficult. Iran has the ability to retaliate, which could involve unleashing terrorism (using Hamas and Hizbollah) against Israel and the

United States and promoting instability in the region, including in Iraq, Afghanistan, and Saudi Arabia. A preventive strike on Iran would also further alienate the Arab and Muslim worlds, where many resent the double standard of American and international acceptance of Israel's and India's nuclear weapons programs. Much of the Iranian population, currently alienated from the regime, could actually rally around it, making external efforts to bring about a change in regime that much more unlikely. Attacking Iran would also lead to sharp and possibly prolonged increases in the price of oil.[17] Launching a preventive war to oust the regime is simply too ambitious; Iran is a country nearly the size of Alaska with 70 million people, roughly three times that of Iraq, and therefore more than enough to make any occupation miserable, costly, and in the end futile. The United States would not avoid these costs were Israel to carry out the strike (a scenario suggested by Vice President Dick Cheney in January 2005), as it would be widely viewed as doing America's bidding.[18]

What is called for is an international proposal to Iran in which it would receive the nuclear fuel it says it requires for power generation but not access to or control of the fuel itself. Such an approach could be made to Iran alone, although it might well stand a better chance of being accepted by the government in Tehran if the offer were put forward as a new global policy in which no government other than the five NPT nuclear weapons states and the IAEA would be permitted control of nuclear fuel. Iran, currently subject to numerous U.S. economic sanctions, could also receive economic benefits and security assurances akin to the sort of package being considered for North Korea. In exchange, and again similar to the case of North Korea, Iran would have to convince the world through inspections that it is not developing nuclear weapons or producing the fuel they would require. The United States needs to reach agreement with Europe, Russia, and others on this package and to threaten Iran with sanctions or other penalties if it were to refuse.[19]

It is possible (some would say likely) that diplomacy would fail, either because of insufficient international support for a package of incentives and penalties or the desire of many in Iran for it to become a nuclear weapons state regardless of the cost. But as in the North Korea case, there is an argument in favor of exploring the diplomatic option, given the costs of carrying out anything more aggressive and given that the only chance for building international support for (or even acceptance of) a more robust approach is to first demonstrate that a good faith effort was made to resolve matters diplomatically. Moreover, and as suggested before, the United States would have a major interest in such a situation to introduce a dimension of deterrence to its policy, making clear to the Iranian government that its existence would be placed in jeopardy if it were found to be transferring nuclear materials to a terrorist organization. In neither the Iranian nor the North Korean case, however, does preventive action look either desirable or doable. As these are likely to remain the two most pressing proliferation challenges for some time to come, U.S. policymakers would be wise to contemplate a strategic future in which preventive action played little or no role.

Despite substantial differences between the United States and other governments over such issues as Iraq, preventive attacks, and how to address the North Korean and Iranian challenges, there is a broad consensus on the desirability of halting further proliferation and on taking steps to tighten up the worldwide set of arrangements designed to make it more difficult to build or acquire nuclear weapons. The opportunity to slow and in some cases prevent the spread of nuclear weapons is real.

But it will not always be possible to prevent further proliferation, much less reverse what has already taken place. When nonproliferation efforts fail, the major powers must have a concerted, well thought out response ready. Nonproliferation policy did not block Israel, India, and Pakistan from becoming nuclear weapons states, and North Korea may be one as well. Iran and possibly others could join their ranks. Since preventive or preemptive strikes are unlikely to provide a remedy, and preventive wars are extraordinarily costly, a collective response is essential. Ballistic missile defense is at most a partial answer: Not only is it uncertain whether it will work, despite the considerable investment, but the most likely threats from nuclear weapons are more likely to arrive in the United States in some container rather than on top of a missile. North Korea and

Iran must be deterred from using nuclear weapons or transferring any nuclear material to third parties. With terrorist groups, however, there is little to be done other than to make it as difficult as possible for them to acquire nuclear material or weapons or to employ them if they do. Policy must consequently center on intelligence, law enforcement, homeland security, and measures to increase the security surrounding nuclear installations and stockpiles in Russia while destruction of the stockpiles is accelerated.

Regime Change

THE DISCUSSION of how best to deal with the challenges posed by the North Korean and Iranian nuclear programs focused on three options: deterrence, diplomacy, and military action. There is in principle a fourth approach, however, that would seek to solve the problem by removing the offending regime and replacing it with a new government that either would not pursue nuclear weapons or, even if it did, would be so different in character that we would not be nearly as concerned by the prospect.

The notion of looking to regime change as a policy panacea is nothing new. Challenges from countries characterized by the pursuit of threatening weaponry and repressive policies at home and abroad is hardly a post–Cold War or post-9/11 phenomenon. The Cold War can in many ways be understood as a prolonged confrontation with a state of precisely this sort—a Soviet Union that threatened the United States by what it did beyond its borders and offended Americans by what it did within them. Earlier in the twentieth century, U.S. struggles with Nazi Germany and Imperial Japan also fit this description.

These historical examples are illuminating, for they begin to suggest the full range of approaches available to the United States in such situations. In the case of Germany and Japan, the policy ultimately chosen by the Roosevelt administration was not simply war in the aftermath of being attacked but regime change, that is, a policy of not simply defeating the enemy on the battlefield and reversing its conquests but continuing war until the regime was ousted and something much different and better was firmly ensconced. The latter objective required years of armed occupation and intrusive involvement in both countries' internal politics until the time arrived when the United States concluded that no threat was forthcoming. The contemporary term for this policy would be nation building.

The Soviet case was markedly different for several reasons. Many Americans were slow to appreciate the full horror of Soviet internal practices. Even then, at the time of World War II, the United States put aside its qualms and concerns about Soviet behavior in order to join ranks against what was judged to be the far greater and more immediate threats emanating from Nazi Germany and Japan. After World War II, though, the Soviet Union emerged as the principal global rival of and threat to the United States and its allies. "Rollback" became something of a popular concept in the 1950s. Yet the potential for a nuclear war in which there would be no winners regardless of who struck first tempered U.S. policy. A policy of regime change or rollback was deemed too risky, even reckless, given what could result if a desperate Soviet leadership lashed out with all the force at its disposal.

But simply acquiescing to Soviet behavior at home and abroad was not a desirable option either. It was George Kennan who produced the intellectual answer of containment in his "long telegram," which ultimately found its way into *Foreign Affairs* in 1947. The thrust of Kennan's recommended approach was clear: "[T]he main element of any United States policy toward the Soviet Union must be that of a long-term, patient but firm and vigilant containment of Russian expansive tendencies." But containment was not as modest as its critics alleged. Less cited is what might be described as its second dimension. "It is entirely possible for the United States to influence by its actions the internal developments, both within Russia and throughout the international Communist movement.... [T]he United States has it in its power to increase enormously the strains under which Soviet policy must operate, to force upon the Kremlin a far greater degree of moderation and circumspection than it has had to observe in recent years, and in this way to promote tendencies which must eventually find their outlet in either the break-up or the gradual mellowing of Soviet power."[20]

As a result, the policy's second, subordinate goal was that of regime change, which it eventually achieved. But this method of regime change is better understood as regime evolution; it necessarily took a back seat to containment and required more than forty years after it was formally introduced. Whereas regime change (in the sense of removal) tends to be direct and immediate and to involve the use of military force or covert action, regime evolution tends to be indirect and gradual and to involve the use of foreign policy tools other than force (although it still may rely in part on covert actions).

Advocates of regime change generally reject most, sometimes any, dealings with the regime in question, lest the process of interaction or engagement somehow buttress the very government whose ouster is sought. Diplomacy is marginalized: This has been the case with U.S. policy toward Cuba for more than four decades. An explicit call for regime change is hardly an approach likely to build an atmosphere conducive to diplomacy: Very few regimes will negotiate their own demise. Regime evolution, however, accepts the need for integration and even give-and-take.

Therefore, it is not surprising that the United States carried out an active diplomacy with the Soviet Union throughout the Cold War. It mattered not whether the policy was characterized minimally as "peaceful coexistence" or somewhat more optimistically as "détente"; either way, the United States was prepared to enter into agreements with the Soviet Union when the agreements were judged on balance to serve U.S. interests. This required two sets of trade-offs. The first: that containment took precedence over rollback or regime change. Second, it meant that influencing Soviet foreign policy took precedence over influencing Soviet behavior at home. This did not mean the United States ignored questions of what was going on inside the Soviet Union—it did not, as evidenced by sustained support for various radio broadcasts meant to speak directly to the Soviet people, by support for individual human rights cases and the right to emigrate—but only that it did not always accord them equal weight. Foreign policy, like all policy, must choose priorities if it is to succeed.

The successful handling of the Soviet Union required interaction. Arms control was one instance. The United States agreed to negotiate with Soviet leaders and enter into agreements to limit their armaments, particularly their nuclear ones. Such a policy arguably prolonged the Soviet regime, as it accorded it a unique and prominent standing and placed curbs on an arms race that would otherwise have proven even more costly and perhaps hastened the demise of a regime built on a weak economic base. Still, avoiding war and regulating U.S.-Soviet arms competition was prudently deemed a higher objective. Similar arguments surrounded U.S. economic dealings with the Soviet Union. There was some risk that such dealings could buttress the Soviet government, but this concern was overridden by the view that it would create a Soviet stake in better relations with the United States and the West and thereby rein in any Soviet inclination to violently challenge the status quo.

In the end, change came to the Soviet Union. Historians

can and will continue to debate the causes: how much was due to Soviet internal flaws, how much was because of U.S. and Western policy. The easy answer is "both." The end did come, and it came peacefully. The third great conflict of the twentieth century, like the first two, ended with the result desired by the United States; unlike the first two, though, the Cold War ended without a total war.[21]

One unexpected byproduct of this outcome is that the United States did not occupy a "defeated" Russia (the principal successor state to the Soviet Union) in the Cold War's wake. Such an option did not exist. Consequently, today's Russia is not as remade as many would have hoped for. Russian democracy is incomplete, to say the least. Countries that are truly defeated and then occupied for years are more pliable to outside engineering than those that do not see themselves as defeated or those that are not fully and deeply occupied for an extended period. Indeed, only with prolonged and intrusive occupation can there be a high expectation of true regime change. This is because regime change, if it is to have any meaning, involves not simply regime ouster but also regime replacement with something demonstrably better and lasting.

The example of the Soviet Union has important consequences for U.S. foreign policy today. The first is that ousting odious leaders and regimes is no easy thing. The Soviet Union survived for nearly three-quarters of a century. Saddam Hussein and the Ba'athist regime in Iraq survived a costly stalemate against Iran and a crushing defeat at the hands of the U.S.-led international coalition in 1991. The

United States found it surprisingly difficult to locate and arrest Manuel Noriega in Panama in 1989; it proved exceedingly costly and in the end impossible to oust Mohammed Farah Aideed in Somalia.

Regime replacement is even more difficult. Ousting Saddam was relatively easy, at least compared with putting into place a functioning government that could run a secure, viable country. Although the Iraq venture was made far more expensive and more difficult than it needed to be because of a lack of careful planning and some questionable decisions (such as dismantling the Iraqi military and the country's governing infrastructure), one cannot assume that things would have gone smoothly had Iraq's occupation been approached differently, or that occupations elsewhere will be much easier.[22] The rise of nationalism together with globalization (and with it the ability to gain access to powerful and effective means of resistance) may have doomed prospects for prolonged occupations, given the sharp rise of the human, military, and economic costs of carrying them out. Those who seek to spread democracy most likely will have to find alternative methods.

These realizations must govern U.S. policy toward North Korea and Iran. The uncertainties surrounding regime change make it an unreliable approach for dealing with specific problems such as a nuclear weapons program. Neither country is on the precipice of dramatic domestic change. A decade ago North Korea was believed by many to be on the brink of collapse; it may well remain on the brink for years to come, notwithstanding its impoverishment, its cruel and eccentric leadership, and its utter lack of freedom. Iran, too, is likely to remain under its current leadership, despite the fact that the clerics ruling the country are unpopular and quietly opposed by a majority of the people. Regime change will not come quickly enough to remove the nuclear threat.

Employing military force to bring about regime change is not a viable option. Using more indirect tools to bring about regime evolution might well work, but this, too, will take years if not decades. We must adjust our expectations to a long-term approach and abandon the fantasy of a quick fix. The tools of regime evolution range from using television and radio and the Internet to bringing countries into the WTO on terms that require fundamental economic and indirectly political reforms. Rhetorical support for change can also help, although it is no substitute for policy. But integration itself can be an important instrument of regime evolution. Economic and political incentives should be made available if policies are adopted that reduce threats posed and that create more freedom and space for independent economic and political activity; in the absence of such changes, targeted sanctions may be appropriate. Trade and exchanges can open a society to new ideas. Over the past few decades we have seen literally dozens of examples of successful regime evolution involving the former Soviet bloc and much of Latin America and Asia; there is no reason such patterns could not be repeated elsewhere if the outside world is prepared to make the in-

vestment and take the necessary time.[23] Odious or dangerous regimes should never be neglected, but the safest and
best way to encourage their modification or even their im-
plosion is to smother them in the policy of integration.

5

•

Economic Integration

Much of this book has focused on efforts to integrate the major powers into cooperative arrangements so that they and the United States can successfully manage the challenges inherent in a global world such as ours. But another dimension of integration involves those who are anything but major powers, namely, the majority of the world's people whose lives tend to be defined by what they lack.

There are three justifications for including this as a foreign policy or national security issue. The first is humanitarian. There is something inherently and fundamentally wrong with human beings not being able to live a full life, given modern advances in health care and food production. And right now there are simply too many men, women, and children who fall into this category.

The second argument is strategic. Societies where poverty prevails or unemployment is widespread are particularly vulnerable to instability and internal conflict, which in turn can lead to immense human hardship or worse. This is one of the lessons to be drawn from the experience in the 1990s with the former Yugoslavia.[1] Societies with weak economies and political systems are also more vulnerable to exploitation by outsiders, be they criminal organizations, drug cartels, or terrorists. Areas where sovereignty is not asserted are vacuums all too easily filled by forces that are anything but benign.

The third argument is economic. Societies defined by high rates of unemployment, a lack of savings, low or no growth, and low per capita GDP tend to be societies that cannot be good trading partners or investment magnets for the United States or anyone else. To the contrary, such places become resource drains, requiring substantial amounts of aid simply to stay afloat and keep people alive.

The argument for doing something to change the status quo in these countries is strong. Inaction is not an option, especially as nothing suggests that things will get better without outside involvement.[2] There are an estimated 3 billion people—half the population of the planet—who subsist at or below the poverty level, defined as $2 a day or less. Roughly 50 percent of the world's poorest people live in China and India; two-thirds are found in just six countries: China, India, Indonesia, Pakistan, Nigeria, and Bangladesh. Thus, the lion's share of the world's poor lives in countries with large populations that are at least partly well off and who as a result do not always qualify for the billions of dollars, euros, and yen of assistance that the wealthier countries make available either directly or through various regional and global institutions.

To assist the poor living in countries such as China and India, the best strategy is promoting policies that boost the overall growth of those economies. The number of poor people tends to go down by 2 percent every time the GDP of a country rises by 1 percent.[3] There are many ideas as to how to generate higher growth rates, but the prevailing one favors such reforms as reducing the degree of government spending and ownership (or increasing private ownership), instituting the rule of law and modern accounting practices along with a fair tax system, rooting out corruption, cutting back on licensing requirements, and, in particular, protecting property rights. Also needed are social structures such as a modern education system and laws that ensure opportunity for girls and women. Many of the reforms that improve the chances of economic success are important elements of promoting democratic reform as well; as a result, political and economic openness tend to be reinforcing. The goal is to create environments that promote productive economic activity and attract foreign investment, since the flows of foreign investment around the world are vast and dwarf flows of aid. Still, countries must compete for investment, which tends to go to the more developed or promising places, not to those countries whose citizens are mostly poor.

Between 500 million and 1 billion people live in countries that are classified as poor. One instrument for addressing persistent poverty is development assistance. The U.S. government gives more than $16 billion a year for this purpose, more than any other country but lower than most wealthy countries if measured as a proportion of national income. The impact of U.S. aid on world poverty is further diluted by the fact that much of the aid goes to disaster relief (rather than to long-term economic development) and to countries that are deemed strategic (such as Egypt, Pakistan, Colombia, and Jordan) rather than to those that are the poorest.[4]

But even higher and better targeted levels of development aid would be no panacea. Increased aid can cause more harm than good if it allows governments to persist in carrying out poor policies and in avoiding painful but necessary reforms.[5] Aid must be conditional on the adoption of specific economic and political reforms. The creation of the Millennium Challenge Account (MCA) is thus a step in the right direction. Announced by President Bush in late 2002, MCA makes several billion dollars of additional development assistance available every year to those countries that adopt "sound" political, economic, and social policies, that is, policies favoring the private sector in societies where there is sufficient transparency and oversight to discourage waste and corruption and where there is a substantial degree of democracy. The additional aid thus becomes both a reward and an incentive for reform. In July 2004, seventy countries were named by the Millennium Challenge Corporation board as candidates to compete for assistance in the coming fiscal year.[6]

But the problem remains: Many of the most destitute countries are unable to qualify, much less successfully compete for the funds. One initiative that is gaining ground (owing mostly to U.S. and U.K. support) is to forgive much or even all of the debt owed by the world's poorest countries (most of which are in Africa) to the World Bank and other international lending institutions. Associated with this initiative is the proposal that new assistance be provided in grants (rather than in loans) to these same countries so as not to create new debt burdens.

Some direct aid is indispensable. Money provided for preventing, treating, or dealing with the consequences of HIV/AIDS and other diseases such as malaria qualifies in this regard. Such aid is not only a humanitarian imperative but is crucial to economic development. No country can thrive if a significant share of its working-age population is too sick to work and if massive amounts of public monies are required for medical care.

But perhaps the most powerful tool in achieving a large-scale lift of millions of people out of poverty is trade. "The opportunity to boost economic growth through increased exports to more open markets may be the most valuable benefit that policies in rich countries can give to the poor in developing countries" is the conclusion of one respected analyst.[7] The decision by the United States and other relatively wealthy countries to phase out tariffs and import quotas for poor country exports of agricultural products, textiles, and apparel and to do the same with export subsidies of their own agricultural products could have a dramatic impact. Literally hundreds of millions of people could move above the poverty line in a decade at only modest cost to the wealthy countries. It is the epitome of integration in action.

Integrating the Haves

TRADE ALSO BRINGS all the countries of the world into a web of relationships that are mutually advantageous economically. The existence of mutually beneficial trading relations acts as an impediment to conflict, as governments are apt to think twice before taking steps that would interrupt or destroy them. Trade thus has an impact on integration that goes beyond the economic.

Trade constitutes a fundamental challenge to the leadership of the major powers and others, however. Regarding genocide, terrorism, and nuclear proliferation, what is at issue for the most part is major power willingness to require others to meet specified standards or behaviors and to collaborate on remedies when the standards are violated. Expressed differently, at issue is major power willingness to take sovereignty away from some other states in certain circumstances. In the case of trade, it is the major powers that must be willing to hold themselves to account and voluntarily cede some aspects of their own sovereignty to the World Trade Organization.

Created in 1995 as the successor to the General Agreement on Tariffs and Trade, the WTO has the mandate to set rules for world trade. No one is required to join the

WTO or compelled to remain a member. Participating (as nearly 150 countries do) in this supranational body with the power to decide trade disputes and insist on remedies is a matter of choice, as is the decision to accept and implement the rulings of WTO judges in specific trade-related disputes. All of this is predicated on the notion that, on balance, operating within such a structured trading system is advantageous for governments even if particular decisions go against them.

The goal of foreign policy in the trade realm is to make international support for the open movement of goods and services across borders as universal as possible. One recent study estimates that U.S. income is $1 trillion per year higher owing to economic integration and could rise by an additional $500 billion per year if global trade were truly free.[8] The reasoning goes back to the basic arguments for free trade: It is a powerful component of economic growth, low inflation, consumer choice, innovation, job creation, development, and productivity gain. This applies as strongly to states that are already wealthy as it does to those that aspire to be.[9]

The classic, economic case for open trade is powerful. It allows countries to specialize in what they do best, which in turn makes their exports competitive and a means for generating wealth. Imports, meanwhile, can supply less expensive goods and services and at the same time introduce new technologies and choice. Trade is associated not so much with job creation per se as with jobs that pay more, because on the average, jobs that are associated with exports pay 10–15 percent more than jobs geared only to the domestic market.

The challenge is to narrow and ultimately end the exceptions or the areas where trade, including agriculture and services, is not open. Tariff and nontariff barriers, including quotas, need to be eliminated, as do price supports. Just as distorting are export subsidies, which make goods and services more competitive than they deserve to be. These, too, need to be phased out.[10]

Each of the major powers has a record that is imperfect. Each at times (some more often than others) is an obstacle to the realization of a truly open world trading system. China is clearly making progress in meeting the commitments it agreed to when it joined the WTO in December 2001. Tariffs have been cut and important areas of its marketplace have been opened. American exports to China have increased to $35 billion a year. But China is deficient in several respects. Intellectual property is often not respected. Joint ventures with foreign firms often encounter all sorts of roadblocks that make it difficult to gain access to parts of the economy such as construction. China's currency is maintained at an artificially low rate against the dollar, which keeps the price of Chinese exports low, giving them a competitive advantage, and makes other countries' exports to China more expensive. This accounts in part for China's huge trade surplus with the United States.

Russia is a different problem. It is not yet a member of the

WTO. It maintains a large number of tariffs that discourage imports. There are as well nontariff barriers (such as sanitary measures and all sorts of licensing requirements) that are effectively trade barriers, making it difficult or impossible for goods to get into Russia or, by demanding special requirements, make them so expensive that they are difficult to sell. Like China, Russia has a poor record of combating piracy of intellectual property. But accession talks between Russia and the WTO are underway—President Vladimir Putin has stated, "We are interested in the further integration of the Russian economy into the international economy, including joining the WTO on conditions that are beneficial to us."[11] Moreover, the growth of Russian-EU trade ties should over time help position Russia to meet WTO requirements and therefore be in a position to join.

India is far more open than it used to be during the decades it flirted with socialism and state-dominated economic policy. India is a member of the WTO, and its trade has grown markedly. But India also maintains high tariff and nontariff walls. Licensing requirements can at times be all but impossible to meet. Certain imports are banned altogether. And it, too, has an unsatisfactory record when it comes to protecting intellectual property.

The single-largest trading partner of the United States is the European Union (although no individual European country can compete with either Canada or Mexico when it comes to bilateral trade with the United States). The EU is a pillar of the WTO. The biggest problem with the EU is its agricultural policies. Massive subsidies give European farmers advantages over those who would like to export to Europe. Subsidies are not limited to agriculture; one U.S. complaint filed in 2004 concerns government subsidies given to Airbus, Europe's large aircraft manufacturer. Also making it difficult for would-be exporters to Europe are nontariff barriers (such as those tied to genetic engineering) that can make it impossible for many American meat and poultry products to enter Europe.

Japan is one of the world's principal trading states and one that mostly lives up to its WTO obligations. There has been progress in persuading Japan to open up to outside investment. The service sector and businesses such as banking and insurance, however, are still difficult to penetrate, and there are subsidies and other advantages for Japanese firms. The biggest problem, though, lies in agriculture and Japan's protection of its farmers through subsidies and barriers to imports.

But overall, since World War II world trade has grown significantly and has made a significant contribution to economic growth and prosperity. The challenge is to sustain growth, which will depend in large part on the ability of the world to conclude a new trade round that takes into account agriculture, services, and the particular needs of the developing countries. Regional and bilateral free trade agreements are no substitute for a global arrangement, as more narrow agreements cannot deal with subsidies and often discriminate against those left out.

In order for this to happen, though, the United States will have to lead. But leading will take more than exhortation. It will also require that the United States set an example. This means making a commitment to phase out or immediately eliminate those remaining aspects of U.S. trade policy that are inconsistent with open trade. This includes tariffs, quotas, price supports, and export subsidies. It also includes production subsidies for agricultural products that cost developing countries billions of dollars a year in lost exports and artificially lowered prices.[12] Such reform is essential if the United States is to be in a position to prevail upon others. The upside of making such a commitment is that it will make possible a new trade round that would redound not just to U.S. but to worldwide benefit.

Trade politics, however, work against the United States behaving in an exemplary fashion. The reason is that those who gain from trade, which is almost everyone, are not always aware of it. The benefits, whether they are lower rates of inflation or greater consumer choice or the existence of an export-dependent job, are often invisible or only partly visible. Those who lose out from trade, however, feel it acutely. Imports are often wrongly blamed for lost jobs, when in fact productivity or technology is the culprit. Although the numbers of those who lose their jobs because of competition are relatively modest, the intensity that these individuals bring to the political process is anything but.

The politics of trade came to a head in 2002, when several U.S. steel producers were facing an uncertain future.

Pressure mounted on the Bush administration to step in to help them. In March 2002, the president imposed tariffs on a variety of steel products for a period of three years, reportedly to give domestic producers breathing space to make changes that would help them better meet international competition. Less than two years later, though, in December 2003, President Bush lifted the tariffs in the face of a WTO ruling that the tariffs were inconsistent with U.S. trade obligations and an EU threat to retaliate. At least as important in the decision to change course were complaints from American steel-using companies whose costs went up, who lost sales and jobs as a result, and who feared the consequences of a European backlash.[13]

A more recent example of trade politics came in 2003 and early 2004 in the form of a debate over outsourcing, the process by which U.S.-based firms give business to firms located overseas that offer lower costs and greater efficiency. Roughly 300,000 American white-collar jobs are being lost a year to this process, and, not surprisingly, there are calls to "do something" about it.

Sometimes, though, "Don't just do something, stand there" can be the best course of action. This is arguably one of them: 300,000 jobs out of a workforce of more than 115 million is a modest percentage. The vast majority of U.S. jobs are locally based and not vulnerable to outsourcing. U.S. firms gain from having access to cheaper and timely but still high-quality services, a benefit that makes them more competitive. Wealth grows overseas, which is good for those U.S. firms that export overseas. Meanwhile, capital that was paying salaries and benefits is freed up and can then be used to create new, higher-value jobs at home.[14]

This does not mean that there are no losers from free trade. There are. Individual firms and workers can lose out to competition. When this happens, and it must, the proper response is not to protect existing jobs (which invariably proves to be expensive and invites retaliation that only decreases the ability of American exports to compete) but rather to provide adjustment assistance to the affected worker. Such assistance can take the form of grants or loans, and makes the most sense if it is aimed not simply to help tide a worker through a difficult transition but also provides the worker with the skills he or she will need to find a new job. Also helpful to individual workers are such things as portable and tax-advantaged health and retirement accounts that are linked to the individual rather than the job. It is important that such benefits be made available to those in the service sector and not just to those in manufacturing.[15]

Lifelong education and retraining is also central to remaining competitive. Given the dynamism of the global economy and the longer span of working lives, the one- or two-job career based on schooling completed by the time a person is in his or her early or mid-twenties is increasingly an anachronism. As one analyst has pointed out, "The future of the U.S. economy does not rest on retaining the jobs now being outsourced, but on the creation of a population with ever-greater skills."[16] If there is reason to be concerned about the future, it is not over current outsourcing but over the state of American education—the poor quality of teaching in math and sciences, the small number of computer science graduates—and the relative lack of resources being devoted to long-term research and development. The outsourcing debate thus touches on two of the themes central to this book and to the opportunity that exists. There is a need for more and not less global economic integration. And to lead this process, the United States must ensure that it has the economic strength and competence to thrive in a competitive global marketplace.

Energy

THE GLOBAL ENERGY market is another manifestation of integration. Here, though, the situation is qualitatively different. The United States is if anything overly integrated into the global energy market, a function of the enormous gap between what the United States produces and what it consumes. Such integration is in effect a costly form of dependence, one that weakens the foundations on which the opportunity is based.

The United States now produces just over 7 million barrels of oil per day. This is a considerable amount, until you view it in the context of what the United States consumes: 20 million barrels of oil a day. The difference has to be made up by imports. Expressed differently, the United States produces nearly 10 percent of the world's oil but consumes 25 percent. The fact that the link between the level of energy use in the United States and economic output (often termed "energy intensity") is lower than it is in most of the world does not alter this reality. The United States also consumes more natural gas than it produces, although the gap here (and the resulting need for imports) is much smaller. Other forms of energy, including coal, nuclear, hydroelectric, wind, and solar, provide only a relatively small percentage of what Americans consume.

High levels of energy use and dependence upon imported energy entail substantial costs to the United States and the American people. High energy costs are a burden on businesses and consumers alike; they absorb resources as would a tax, contribute to inflation, and make U.S. goods more expensive and hence less attractive overseas. High energy costs also contribute to the fiscal deficit: The U.S. government is a major user of energy. Energy imports also contribute to the U.S. current account (essentially trade) deficit, thereby adding to U.S. economic vulnerability and putting pressure on the dollar. The current situation requires that the United States transfer considerably more than $100 billion a year to others to pay for the energy it imports. This constitutes nearly 10 percent of the total trade deficit. There is as well the environmental consideration. The use of oil, natural gas, and coal exacerbates global warming; one can debate the extent of climate change, but one cannot seriously debate that climate change is taking place and that its consequences will on balance be decidedly adverse for most Americans.[17]

American energy dependence also distorts U.S. foreign policy and national security. Arguably even more important than vulnerability to price increases is vulnerability to supply interruption. Instability in some parts of the world is a matter of humanitarian concern; instability in critical oil-producing areas jeopardizes the American and world economies. What takes place in the broader Middle East and in some other countries matters far more than it otherwise would, were the United States and the world far less dependent upon Middle East oil and gas exports.

Unfortunately, oil and gas are often found in countries where stability and production cannot be taken for granted. Nearly two-thirds of the world's known oil and gas is found in the greater Middle East and in countries such as Saudi Arabia, Iran, Iraq, the United Arab Emirates, Kuwait, and Libya. Other large producers include Venezuela (a country run by someone who can hardly be described as a friend of the United States and where oil fields suffer from frequent labor stoppages); Russia (a country where the government and the oil-producing firms are often at odds); and Nigeria (a country experiencing varying degrees of civil strife). Given the close balance between global supply and demand, even a modest interruption in production anywhere could have significant economic consequences for the United States and the world.

One mechanism that exists to mitigate the consequences of supply disruptions is the International Energy Agency. Created in 1974, the IEA now includes the United States and twenty-five other countries. Each is required to maintain oil stocks equivalent to at least 90 days of net imports and, in the event of an oil supply disruption of 7 percent or more to the IEA overall or to an individual country, to release oil stocks, restrain domestic demand, switch to the extent possible to other fuels, increase domestic oil production, and share oil with other IEA members. This is one area where the world has usefully integrated in the energy realm—in part to offset the cartel of the Organization of Petroleum Exporting Countries (OPEC), a more narrow form of integration that serves the interests of its members but not the larger international community.

The United States is right to pursue a policy of supply diversification. It makes sense to produce oil in as many countries as possible and to import oil from as many countries as possible. Such physical or geographical diversity reduces the impact of supply interruptions from any one source, although an interruption from Saudi Arabia (the world's largest producer by far) would have enormous impact. There are limits to such a strategy, though, given where oil and gas fields are concentrated.

Some people argue for increasing world energy supplies. More oil and gas and more energy in general, it is said, helps keep prices down and again is a cushion against loss of supply from any single source. But expanding production is very expensive and, again, the most promising areas for exploration tend to be in those same countries that already account for the lion's share of world production. We would increase our dependence upon them. The gains that would come from opening up the Arctic National Wildlife Refuge in Alaska would be modest and would not change the facts about where the United States gets its energy.[18] What is more, world demand for oil and gas will continue to rise as China, India, and other countries become more and more developed and industrially active. It will take a great deal for supply to keep up with demand; the hope that oil and gas supplies could come to greatly exceed demand (and thereby reduce prices and render the United States and the rest of the world less vulnerable to the effects of any production disruption) is extremely remote.

Any energy strategy worthy of the name must therefore aim to reduce demand and to lower energy use, and above all, oil and gas use. This is the only way to reduce the financial, strategic, and environmental costs of current policy. Some of this can come from a second form of energy diversification, namely, developing alternative sources of energy. Meaningful results will only come about if politics evolve (making it possible to build new nuclear plants) and if the investment is adequate and the technology proves viable.

Against such uncertain ambitions is the guaranteed potential for increasing energy efficiency and reducing energy use.[19] This can be done without adversely affecting the U.S. economy. Energy efficiency has improved in the past without compromising economic growth; one study states that between 1977 and 1985, U.S. oil consumption declined by 17 percent while GDP climbed 27 percent.[20] What it would require are changes in U.S. law, beginning with changing the provision that classifies SUVs as light trucks outside federal laws that mandate higher levels of fuel efficiency. Raising requirements for fuel efficiency across the board would have a similar effect. Higher gasoline taxes are another means of reducing consumption; if this is deemed to be politically unacceptable, incentives can be used to induce Americans to purchase hybrid cars or other cars that offer much higher fuel efficiency.

Energy policy highlights many of the themes of this book. The world is highly integrated, but the United States must work with other countries to protect itself from the adverse aspects of globalization. Maintaining order in energy-producing regions is a high priority. But even more important is taking steps that ensure American strength, which in this domain actually argues for reducing U.S. vulnerability to globalization. Energy dependency has become an Achilles heel for the United States; that said, the opportunity exists to do something about it, an opportunity that if exploited will yield a trifecta of economic, environmental, and national security dividends.

6

•

The Other Major Powers

I T I S N O T O N L Y the United States that has a stake in seeing the emergence of a highly integrated world. The other major powers are similarly vulnerable to the threats posed by globalization and are in even less of a position to meet them alone. Nor are they in any position to challenge the United States directly. What they do need is an extended period of international stability so that they can focus on economic development and growth (in the case of China, Russia, India, and Japan) and political development (in the case of Europe). Good ties with the United States are an essential dimension of this.

"China and the United States are destined to be adversaries as China's power grows" is the prediction of one respected analyst.[1] Such speculation is unmerited. China's GDP is roughly half that of the United States, but given its large population, its GDP per capita is only $5,000, one-seventh or one-eighth that of the United States. (It makes sense to think of China's large population of 1.3 billion as constituting as much of a burden as it does a resource.)

China spends some $60 billion on its military, roughly 15 percent the amount the United States does. Vast stretches of China, including hundreds of millions of people living in rural agricultural areas, remain quite poor and underdeveloped. A large gap persists between China's often booming economy and a political system that is top-heavy and having trouble (in the case of the Communist Party) making the case for its own continued relevance.

For their part, China's leaders have accentuated the need for decades of stability so that China can focus its attention on economic growth. Consistent with this emphasis has been the articulation in recent years of the "peaceful rise" doctrine for China at this stage of its history. This doctrine (possibly superseded by the formulation "peaceful development") is meant to signal China's neighbors that China's burgeoning economic power (and its growing military might) will not be used in an effort to assert hegemony in the region. China does not want to alienate its neighbors or the United States; nor does it want to divert the lion's share of its human and financial resources to the military sector and away from more productive investments. China requires a benign environment that will allow it to export manufactured goods, import energy and foreign investment, and avoid a costly arms race or conflict that would divert resources and disrupt the very trade and investment flows fueling China's development.[2]

Russia is in much the same situation, and perhaps even more so. Russia is a major power in name only. Although it possesses vast territory, bountiful natural resources, a seat on the UN Security Council, and a stockpile of nuclear weapons that rivals that of the United States, in other respects Russia is anything but powerful. It is a country with a shrinking population of some 145 million (now smaller than Pakistan's) and a GDP roughly the size of Brazil's. Russia's male population is being decimated by alcoholism and HIV/AIDS, and the health care system meant to care for them is in a shambles. Russia's future prominence, even its viability, cannot be taken for granted.

Russian leaders, like China's, seem to have determined that the only way for Russia to recover its great power status in more than symbolic terms involves economic transformation, which in turn requires prolonged stability both at home and abroad and a good working relationship with the United States. Russian president Vladimir Putin made this clear in his end-of-year (December 23, 2004) press conference: "The United States is one of our priority partners. We have implemented a great deal of joint projects in the economic sphere. We are, undoubtedly, partners in addressing a series of pressing modern-day issues, above all in countering terrorism. I would even say we are more than partners, we are allies in this sphere."

There remain important differences between China and Russia, on the one hand, and the United States, on the other, when it comes to specific issues and opinions on how the world is to be organized and run. In a 2001 treaty, for example, China and Russia agreed to combine efforts to maintain "a global strategic balance. . . ."[3] This can be read as an expression of concern about American preeminence. Yet this statement is more noteworthy for what it does not say: There is no direct criticism of the United States. Nor is there much substance to the Sino-Russian relationship, which in no way resembles an alliance or a classic effort to counter American power and reach. Russia and China cannot afford to be America's adversaries—and they know it.

India is closer still to the United States. To begin with, India (unlike both China and Russia) is a bona fide democracy. While never quite a foe of the United States during the Cold War, India (its professions of nonalignment notwithstanding) was more often than not aligned with the Soviet Union against the United States. The end of the Cold War has made these debates obsolete; consistent with this, and reinforced by both a determination to join and benefit from the global economy and a nearly 2-million strong Indian-American community, India has to a considerable degree jettisoned the reflexive anti-Americanism that characterized its foreign policy for much of the Cold War. The change is such that Prime Minister Manmohan Singh now speaks of there being "a mutuality of interest and a complementarity of major objectives" that provides a basis for a durable U.S.-Indian partnership devoted to "the building of a stable, secure, prosperous, and equitable world order."[4] That is the language of a country that seeks integration as a major power.

India needs to focus on economic growth because although it has the world's largest middle class, it also has more poor people than any other single country. As a result, per capita GNP is less than $3,000 a year, approximately $1,000 below Russia's and $2,000 below that of China. India also has a population that within a few decades will overtake China's and become the world's largest. All this suggests a need for sustained economic growth near or at levels as high as 8–10 percent, something that can be attained only if India attracts American capital and technology and has access to the American market.

It is noteworthy that the attitudes of Japan and Europe, the two members of a potential concert that also happen to be allies of the United States, are more complex than those of China, Russia, and India. This should not be all that surprising, as it is allies who must undergo the difficult adaptation to the loss of the rationale or impetus that originally brought them together when one geopolitical era gives way to another.[5]

But there are important differences between Japan and Europe. The Cold War may have ended and the Soviet Union may no longer exist, but most Japanese still see the world as a dangerous place and the United States as a useful friend. Japan directly faces the uncertainty over a North Korea that is developing nuclear weapons and testing missiles that can reach Tokyo. There are as well unresolved territorial disputes with Russia and the challenge of a rising China. Against this backdrop, Japan's hesitancy to associate itself closely with the United States has less to do with anti-Americanism (although there is certainly some of it) than it does with an unresolved internal debate over Japan's role in the world and to what extent it should remain a special case because of its World War II legacy of armed aggression. The prevailing trend, though, is clear: for Japan to become more active in the world and more than a one-dimensional economic power.[6]

Europe is arguably the most complicated would-be partner of the United States. Europe has embarked on a historic process of what can best be described as its own integration. Indeed, Europe's experience over the past half century constitutes a remarkable (and hopeful) example of how countries can come together and cooperate despite past animosity and present inequality. This is not meant to suggest, however, that what is taking place in Europe is a model for anywhere else. Europe's integration is too intimate and too bureaucratic (and too much a result of its unique history) to serve as a paradigm for other regions, much less for the world as a whole.

The fact that the U.S.-European relationship is experiencing turbulence is not surprising. That is nothing new. Transatlantic ties were often stormy during the Cold War, as is suggested by the title of Henry Kissinger's landmark book, *The Troubled Partnership*.[7] Still, there is something different about current problems. The end of the Cold War and the disappearance of the Soviet threat removed the glue that provided the essential rationale for the military alliance. Once America and Europe no longer needed to assert a common anti-Communist front, they were free to explore their differences. These have proved easy to find. Generational change has had an impact; for Europeans under the age of sixty, the United States is less the popular country that liberated the continent during World War II than the controversial leader of a coalition that attacked Iraq and rejects both the International Criminal Court and the Kyoto Protocol. Differences on social issues (including capital punishment, abortion, and drug policy) further exacerbate tensions across the Atlantic. Even Europe's success may be a source of difficulty, in that many Europeans naturally see the world through a lens framed by their own recent experience, whereas Americans often see the world in somewhat more combative terms. One perceptive French observer has even suggested that we have gone from a Cold War configuration of one West and two Europes to a current world of one Europe but two Wests.[8]

Recent history is not a one-sided saga of drifting apart, however. In 1990, soon after the Cold War came to a sudden end and in the wake of Iraq's invasion and occupation of Kuwait, Europeans and Americans joined to resist and ultimately to reverse Saddam Hussein's aggression. Throughout that same decade, Americans and Europeans managed to bridge their differences and collaborated to protect the populations of both Bosnia and Kosovo. More recently, they have found a way to enlarge and reorient NATO, to make it more difficult for terrorists to carry out their activities, and to stabilize Afghanistan in the aftermath of the war there.

The rationale for U.S.-European cooperation is strong. Both the United States and Europe (Europe arguably more, given its relative weakness) need the other to meet the common challenges of globalization and to take advantage of its benefits. There is much the United States will need to do and, in some instances, concede. But no less a prerequisite for transatlantic cooperation is that Europeans resist the temptation to define themselves in terms of opposition to the United States. There are three competing ideas as to Europe's role in the world: Europe as partner of the United States, Europe as balancer of the United States, and Europe as an island, a region that mostly opts out of difficult international undertakings and focuses on the quality of life on the continent. Although the second and third choices are more rhetorical than real—despite periodic French calls for a multipolar world, Europeans lack the means for the second and would be naive to believe the third would provide viable security—the triumph of the first choice (championed by U.K. prime minister Tony Blair) is by no means assured. The challenge for American foreign policy is to work so that this first option, Europe as partner, wins out. It is no less a challenge for responsible Europeans to see that this happens. The transatlantic partnership can and must prevail. It is reassuring that the EU's main statement on security makes a point along these lines: "The transatlantic relationship is irreplaceable. Acting together, the European Union and the United States can be a formidable force for good in the world. Our aim should be an effective and balanced partnership with the USA."[9] But the statement needs to be matched with deeds, and with a careful nurturing of popular opinion in Europe by European leaders. The partnership is too vital to play politics with.

American Choices

THE GOVERNMENTS of the world's principal powers will cooperate with the United States only if there is a context in which their fundamental national interests are seen by their own publics to be protected. Integration will not get far if it is judged to only or even mostly serve U.S. interests, even if these interests happen to be largely consistent with those of other countries. The priorities of these governments must also be addressed.

For China, the preeminent issue is Taiwan. China does not regard this as a foreign policy issue but as an internal matter that is at the core of its identity as a nation-state. China sees Taiwan as an integral part of the country; the only question for China's leaders and its people is when and how reunification will come about.

The United States does not directly challenge the notion of a single Chinese political entity that includes Taiwan. The Nixon administration agreed to this in February 1972 in the so-called Shanghai Communiqué, which set forth the basis for relations between Washington and Beijing (then Peking): "The United States acknowledges that all Chinese on either side of the Taiwan Strait maintain there is but one China and that Taiwan is a part of China. The United States Government does not challenge that position." Every U.S. administration since, Republican and Democratic alike, has reiterated this basic mantra, underscoring its position by maintaining formal diplomatic relations only with the mainland.

At the same time, the United States maintains obligations to Taiwan (the Republic of China), the island remnant of Nationalist (non-Communist) China. These obligations are enshrined in the Taiwan Relations Act of 1979, and state that "the United States decision to establish diplomatic relations with the People's Republic of China rests upon the expectation that the future of Taiwan will be determined by peaceful means" and that it is U.S. policy to maintain the capacity "to resist any resort to force or other forms of coercion that would jeopardize the security, or the social or economic system, of the people of Taiwan." The act also includes a requirement that "the United States will make available to Taiwan such defense articles and defense services in such quantity as may be necessary to enable Taiwan to maintain a sufficient self-defense capability." Consistent with these obligations, the United States has become Taiwan's principal source of arms, providing it with literally billions of dollars' worth over the years.

For more than three decades the United States has sought—successfully for the most part—to balance this set of competing if not contradictory commitments. China has been discouraged from employing military force to unify the country; Taiwan's rulers have been discouraged from declaring independence or taking steps tantamount to such a declaration that would have the potential effect of triggering a military response from the mainland. Mainland China cannot dismiss the possibility that any use of military force on its part would meet with a U.S. military response; leaders in Taiwan cannot be sure they can count on U.S. assistance, particularly if it is some provocative action by Taiwan that alters the status quo that is the proximate cause of any crisis.

This policy of "deterrence through uncertainty" is beginning to wear thin, however. Taiwan, ever more democratic, is inching in the direction of independence. For years there was consensus in Taiwan that there was only one China and that the government in Taipei rather than the one in Beijing constituted the legitimate government; now, increasingly, Taiwan's leaders are putting forward what amounts to a two-China policy. Meanwhile, the People's Republic of China has been steadily building up the military might it could bring to bear against Taiwan at the same time it regularly issues warnings and sends signals that it will not tolerate Taiwan's independence.[10]

The administration of George W. Bush rightly warned Taiwan's leaders not to go too far in the direction of independence. Speaking on December 9, 2003, in the presence of visiting Chinese premier Wen Jiabao, President Bush stated, "We oppose any unilateral decision by either China or Taiwan to change the status quo, and the comments and actions made by the leader of Taiwan indicate that he may be willing to make decisions unilaterally, to change the status quo, which we oppose. . . . The United States policy is one China." Implicit in this rebuke of Taiwan's leadership is the view that self-determination is not and cannot be a universal right. We have come a long way since the post–World War II colonial era, when the claim to an independent state by many was relatively straightforward; by contrast, virtually all of today's candidate states (including Kurdistan, Palestine, and Tibet) would trigger a war by unilateral assertions of independence, face real questions of viability, or both. To borrow from the Camp David Accord, which in addition to setting the terms of peace between Israel and Egypt lays out principles for addressing the demands of Palestinian nationalism in a context of maintaining Israel's security, Taiwan has the right to participate in the determination of its own future, but not to determine it alone.

There is some irony in all this, for patience on the part of Taiwan's leaders would likely be rewarded in that the mainland is gradually becoming more open and hence more like Taiwan. Reunification that brings about a China that resembles Taiwan more than the mainland is thus possible with the passage of time. But it is not clear that Taiwan's leaders will accept this. If Taiwan were to cross a clear red line—such as by formally declaring itself to be a separate, sovereign state—it is important that it not be recognized. It should also face economic and political sanctions. At the same time, the mainland should be strongly discouraged from using military force, an objective that requires the United States not to rule out acting in Taiwan's defense and backing that up with credible forces. The goal should be to deal with the crisis short of war and return to the situation as it now stands.

If the mainland were to use military force, it should not be allowed to successfully reunify the country. Allowing it to do so would set a terrible precedent for the region and beyond. It could trigger a wave of rearmament and even nuclear proliferation, as a number of governments in the area would reflexively fear China and question American reliability. Still, if China were to use force and war were to occur, it should be waged in a manner designed to keep it as limited as possible in both weaponry and targets. Allowing any confrontation to escalate into a general conflict between the United States and China would be a catastrophe. Nor should the result be any change in the political status of Taiwan; the United States should continue to oppose both reunification by force and independence. The goal is to avoid tempting Taiwan to start a crisis (or rewarding it if it does) and, at the same time, to avoid earning the permanent enmity of 1.3 billion mainland Chinese.

All of this is far easier said than done, so the immediate priority must continue to be preventing any such crisis from materializing. One way to do this would be to communicate the positions and policies described above to both China and Taiwan so that there is no misunderstanding. Deterrence can at times be better promoted through clarity and certainty than through vagueness and uncertainty. The United States should do all it can to encourage economic and transportation links as well as regular dialogue between China and Taiwan. Taiwan could bring the United States and China into armed conflict. More than any other issue, it threatens the existing opportunity to integrate China into a U.S.-led world order, to remake international relations in the twenty-first century, and to build the foundation of a lasting peace.

The enormous imbalance of bilateral trade in China's favor—$162 billion in 2004 alone—also has the potential to undermine prospects for Sino-American cooperation and China's integration if the United States were to adopt protectionist policies in response. Here it is important not to react to the bilateral numbers, which reflect everything from China's stage of development to the high value of the dollar relative to the renminbi, the Chinese currency. A bilateral deficit with China would matter far less if it were offset by U.S. trade surpluses with other countries. U.S. government officials and Congress should focus on ensuring that U.S. exports enjoy fair opportunity and that China is acting in conformity with its WTO obligations. To the extent possible, trade concerns should be "de-bilateralized" and dealt with by the WTO.

Americans would be wise as well to take a long view of the evolution of China's political system. China's politics are still heavily steered from above; that said, the society is far more open today than it was fifteen years ago at the time of the Tiananmen Square crackdown. It is likely to be more open still in the years ahead. The best way to promote this evolution may be to continue to support China's economic opening and programs that strengthen the rule of law. Helping China develop this infrastructure is likely to be far more significant than high-decibel criticisms of China's human rights record.

Russia makes a different set of demands on the United States. How well it provides for the security of its own nuclear weapons and materials, how responsibly it acts to contain the nuclear capabilities of both Iran and North Korea, how it acts vis-à-vis former republics of the Soviet Union that Russia views as constituting its "near abroad"— all can and will have an impact on the interests and objectives that matter most to the United States. There are limits to what Russia can do in the world in a positive sense, but its potential to be a spoiler is considerable.

In dealing with Russia, Americans need to be cognizant of Russia's historic sense of itself as an important power. The United States must treat Russia respectfully, especially in relations with countries that were formerly part of the Soviet Union and now constitute Russia's "near abroad." The United States should not treat these areas as within any Russian sphere of influence—the Bush administration was right to back Ukraine's right to free and fair elections in late 2004—but it should take legitimate Russian concerns into account. The United States should think twice before establishing military bases in those countries near Russia, something to be wary of anyway, given the autocratic and at times corrupt politics that characterize some of these countries. Except in rare circumstances, the United States should not repeat the Cold War pattern of overlooking the domestic nature of countries simply because they associate themselves with us in the struggle against terrorism.

The United States would be wise, too, to keep in mind the commercial focus of much of Russian foreign policy. Despite the surge in oil and gas prices, the Russian economy is fragile; the search for profits sharply shapes policy. When it comes to Iran, for example, it makes little sense for the United States to insist that Russia refuse to sell a nuclear reactor. Instead, the United States should simply work with Russia so that Russia or the international community retains control of any nuclear fuel provided and takes steps to minimize any benefits that would spill over into Iran's own nuclear weapons program.

The United States should not isolate Russia. NATO enlargement was a policy that could have deeply alienated Russia. Fortunately, it did not. One way to make sure that it does not down the road is to involve Russia more and more in what NATO does. Russia is already a member of the Partnership for Peace, a collection of some thirty countries established in 1994 to prepare European countries for possible NATO membership or, failing that, to improve their military capabilities so that they would be in a position to collaborate with NATO. There is also the Russia-NATO Council, a special consultative body established in 2002 to reduce friction between the activities of an enlarged NATO and a sensitive Russia. In the future, Russian membership in NATO should not be precluded if this is something that Russia comes to desire and if it meets NATO's criteria, including that any country wishing to join be sufficiently democratic. NATO is fundamentally different today than it was when it was founded. It has helped former members of the Eastern bloc modernize and democratize, and there is no reason it could not have a similar effect upon Russia. In addition, NATO is less and less a defense organization designed to protect the territory of its members from an aggressive state or alliance along the lines of the Soviet Union or Warsaw Pact. To the extent NATO remains in the collective defense business, it is mostly in the context of defending against terrorism carried out by nonstate actors such as al Qaeda. The first and only time that NATO invoked the "attack on one is an attack on all" commitment was in the aftermath of the 9/11 terrorist attacks on the United States. NATO is increasingly a collective security organization (Article IV, in NATO parlance) whose real purpose is to meet security challenges outside the treaty area, that is, beyond Europe in such countries as Afghanistan (where NATO troops now assume a meaningful role) or Iraq (where they should). Such missions tend to be discretionary, in that they involve some but not all of NATO's twenty-six members. The same could easily hold for Russia, were it to become a member.

More important than integrating Russia into NATO, though, would be integrating it into the world economy. The WTO is one such mechanism. Russia is in the process of negotiating its so-called accession agreement with the WTO. (Each aspiring member must first reach agreement with WTO officials and member states on a timetable for coming into compliance with WTO requirements.) Another and potentially even more valuable link would be to tie Russia to the EU. An EU-Russia free trade agreement building on the May 2004 trade pact makes a good deal of sense in this regard. Obviously, this is not something the United States can determine, but both Russia and the Europeans ought to be left in no doubt that the United States views this relationship as constructive and supports its evolution.

As is the case with China, there is the question of how prominently internal developments in Russia should figure in the U.S. calculus and how the United States should pursue its objectives. This is particularly pertinent given Russia's ongoing war with Chechen rebels and the reduction of civil society, corporate independence, and political checks and balances that are increasingly a characteristic of Vladimir Putin's rule.

All the reasons to promote democratic reform apply in Russia. Beyond the "in principle" argument that democracies are inherently desirable because they provide more protection of individual rights and opportunities, there is the historical record suggesting that mature democracies, those with numerous checks and balances that make it difficult for popular or populist passions to carry the day, make for better international citizens than tyrannies, which tend to be prone to aggression. But it is not easy for Americans or any outsider to promote, much less impose, democratic reform in Russia or anywhere else. Establishing a firm market-economy foundation and the rule of law is likely to pay off over time. Demanding that a country meet all political standards as a prerequisite for full engagement denies the use of engagement and integration as a mechanism for helping a country meet higher standards.

The United States should also respond to legitimate Russian interests, such as Russia's territorial unity. The Chechens have no inherent right to self-determination. Russian leaders are understandably opposed to setting a precedent for secession. There is also the matter of priorities. It makes little sense for the United States to make its larger relationship with Russia, including, say, Russia's policy toward Iran's nuclear program, hostage to what Putin does domestically. The United States does not have the luxury of conducting a foreign policy toward Russia that is solely or even mostly concerned with promoting democracy any more than it does toward China, given the importance of enlisting China in efforts to deal with the North Korean nuclear challenge.

Good foreign policy is not and cannot be an all-or-nothing proposition. It is possible to be sensitive to the Russian desire to maintain national unity at the same time it is possible and important to be critical of Russia's physical methods and its lack of a concerted diplomatic track in Chechnya. Russia should not be allowed a dominant, much less exclusive, sphere of influence in Ukraine or elsewhere in the former "Soviet space." Similarly, American officials (along with those of other democratic countries) can and should be critical of Putin's consolidation of power, as are many prominent Russians. Such criticism is right in principle, lends legitimacy to U.S. efforts to promote democracy elsewhere, and can provide some resistance to Putin's going too far. It would not be wise, though, to introduce sanctions or make cooperation elsewhere dependent on what Russia does in this realm. Compartmentalization can be good advice in political as well as human relationships.

Integrating India would seem to be a relatively straightforward prospect, given the fact that India is a sturdy democracy and a natural strategic partner that is increasingly tied economically to the world. There is also a thriving Indian-American community. Reality (as it invariably does) turns out to be more complicated.

The end of the Cold War provided an opportunity to move beyond all this, and the growth of economic ties between India and the United States has provided real ballast to efforts to integrate India. By 2004, U.S.-Indian trade had reached some $18 billion a year, up from $7 billion a decade earlier. U.S. direct foreign investment in India, in the range of $250 million a year, is considerable, although an order of magnitude below that in China. Still, there are three issues that require attention if India's integration is to realize its potential.

The first involves India's nuclear weapons. India exploded a "peaceful nuclear device" in 1974 and then tested several warheads in 1998, but it is not recognized as one of the five nuclear weapons states by the Nuclear Non-Proliferation Treaty. India has never signed the treaty, seeing it as inherently discriminatory. There is no chance that India will agree to roll back its nuclear weapons program so long as the United States, Russia, China, Great Britain, and France hold onto theirs. The fact that Pakistan also has nuclear weapons only makes the prospect of Indian denuclearization that much more remote.

Integration argues for accepting this state of affairs. This does not require trying to formally amend the treaty itself, an effort that would open up all sorts of insoluble controversies and in the end prove more trouble than it was worth. But the United States must accept the reality that India is a nuclear power and work with India not simply to stabilize its nuclear relationship with Pakistan but also to make India a member of all the arrangements created to frustrate further proliferation to other states or terrorist groups. It also means dropping economic sanctions (as the Bush administration did to a large extent in the fall of 2004) introduced at the time of India's 1998 nuclear test. There is some price to be paid for this concession to reality, in that it reinforces the perception that our approach to the spread of nuclear weapons is inconsistent. Well, the truth is that it is! U.S. policy has been discriminatory from day one, in that the NPT itself recognizes that five countries but not others are entitled (at least temporarily) to possess nuclear weapons.

The United States has also tolerated Israel's nuclear weapons, bowing both to reality but also to a sense that Israel has a claim to such weapons, given the threats and hostility it has faced from most of the Arab world throughout its entire existence. Although it is right to oppose the emergence of new nuclear weapons states in all circumstances, it is also right to oppose it more in some than in others. The character and behavior of the regime—its record of aggression, its history of supporting terrorism, its stability, its record on preventing exports of sensitive technologies, whether it is a democracy, its involvement in a dispute with a neighbor that could lead to a conflict that in turn could involve nuclear weapons—all can and should influence the intensity of U.S. and world opposition to proliferation and what the United States and other countries should be prepared to do to prevent or counter it. While the emergence of a nuclear Iran and a nuclear Switzerland would both be of concern, they would not be of equal concern.

Integrating India will also require that the United States support the notion that India is in fact a major power. Some of this can be accomplished bilaterally, but it also requires supporting India's desire to become a permanent member of the UN Security Council. It is politically hard to reform the Security Council, which only reinforces the argument that the United States and others unequivocally back the understandable aim of India, soon to be the world's most populous country, to join.

What follows is the need to treat India as a major country in its own right and not simply as part of "India-Pakistan." India can and should be invited to certain international meetings even if Pakistan is not. But both India and the United States have an enormous stake in what happens in and to Pakistan: India will never realize its potential if its resources are diverted to contending with Pakistan. Beyond the problem of dealing with Pakistani-supported terrorism, war of any sort and nuclear war in particular would be a catastrophe; India, with a population that includes 150 million Muslims, also has to be mindful about the domestic consequences of heightened tension between mostly Hindu India and Muslim Pakistan. This argues for the United States and the other major powers to do what they can to bolster stability within Pakistan and to support the gradual normalization of relations between India and Pakistan. But the two countries are not, and should not be seen as, equal. India is ready and willing to assume the role of a major power; Pakistan, despite its recent economic progress, is not yet on a trajectory that ensures success.

Japan and the United States have no major issues to overcome. Japan is fully integrated in the world economically. Japan is a signatory of all the principal international counterterrorist conventions and a full participant in efforts to stop money laundering. It is a member of the Proliferation Security Initiative and, given its own history, requires no lessons from anyone on the destructive power of nuclear weapons. Japan is the second-largest financial contributor to the United Nations (after the United States) and maintains the fourth-largest defense budget in the world, despite a constitutional provision that precludes its maintaining land, sea, and air forces.

If there is evidence of Japanese dissatisfaction, it is related to its not being a permanent member of the UN Security Council; as with India, this is something the United States should press to change. The bigger question with Japan, though, concerns its own internal politics and the country's willingness to assume a larger international role that goes beyond being a checkbook for the initiatives of the United States and others. The principal impediment to Japan's assuming a role commensurate with its talents and resources has been Article 9 of its constitution (in which the Japanese people "forever renounce war as a sovereign right") and strong popular and elite resistance to anything that smacks of renewed militarism.

Gradually, however, Japan's leaders have been stretching the boundaries of what is acceptable. Japan, for example, has led the international effort to provide economic support to the government of Afghanistan. It also sent naval forces to the Indian Ocean to provide fuel and other logistical support for U.S. and other military forces participating in Operation Enduring Freedom in Afghanistan. Perhaps most significant, given the absence of a clear international or UN mandate, Japan provided various forms of support to U.S. and international efforts in Iraq, including some 1,000 soldiers participating on the ground and billions of dollars in aid for the reconstruction effort. More generally, Japan has dispatched personnel to eight UN peacekeeping operations and five international relief operations. This sort of involvement that represents a more active, even assertive Japan ought to be encouraged and welcomed. The danger of renewed Japanese militarism is marginal; Japan's capacity to be a significant regional and global partner of the United States is considerable.

Implicit in all of this is the importance of maintaining a good working relationship and strategic partnership with Japan. Asia is clearly the most dynamic region of the world. It remains to be seen whether all this dynamism can be effectively and peacefully harnessed. History suggests that successful economic powers often cannot resist the temptation to see this strength manifested in the political and military realms. Avoiding an Asian arms race will not be easy, given the actual and potential economic growth of China and others, the relative paucity of local institutions with the capacity to manage political and military rivalries (Asia has nothing like what Europe has), the existence of disputes and tensions that go back decades, and the potential for instability or even war stemming from North Korea's nuclear program and the Taiwan question. The United States stands a much better chance of managing this future if it retains close ties to Japan and remains sensitive to Japan's insecurities, which stem from both North Korea's nuclear and missile efforts and from China's rise. What should be avoided at all costs is a sense in Japan that it is essentially on its own, a perception that could lead it over time to accommodate China, turn inward, or even consider assuming a far more assertive or even aggressive role for itself in the region.[11]

Integrating Europe fully into international efforts to meet today's challenges might prove as difficult as any other challenge. Europe cannot be invited onto the UN Security Council as long as France and Britain retain their national seats, which neither is about to give up. Still, this should not get in the way of raising the level and frequency of U.S.-EU consultations on strategic as well as economic issues. It also makes sense for the United States and selected European states to consult closely on the major issues before them.

There has been a debate in American policy circles about how the United States should react to and relate to Europe's greater "collectivism" in the foreign and defense realms. Some have been less than welcoming, fearing that a more united and capable Europe would be more likely to go its own way and work against the United States. One recent book went so far as to argue that "a more closely in-tegrated Europe is no longer an unqualified American interest."[12] This concern is fundamentally misplaced. It is better to have a stronger Europe that sometimes goes its own way in directions the United States questions than a weak Europe that is in no position to be a meaningful partner even if it were so disposed. Secretary of State Condoleezza Rice made just this point in a speech in Paris in 2005: "[A] global agenda requires a global partnership. . . . That is why the United States, above all, welcomes the growing unity of Europe. America has everything to gain from having a stronger Europe as a partner in building a safer and better world."[13]

The real question in this regard is less U.S. policy than it is European will. The twenty-five members of the EU collectively spend more than $160 billion annually on defense. But the whole is considerably less than the sum of its parts; there is too much overlap and too little coordinated specialization. As the principal EU document on Europe's security strategy admits, "Systematic use of pooled and shared assets would reduce duplications, overheads, and, in the medium term, increase capabilities."[14] In addition, there is also too little thought being given to what international roles Europe could usefully assume, such as taking the lead in providing police and military forces to deal with the sort of internal instability that has emerged as a cardinal feature of the contemporary world.

This does not mean that the United States should place a premium on European unity ahead of actual cooperation in particular circumstances. Where there is no consensus within Europe—something increasingly likely to be the case now that the EU has expanded to twenty-five countries and over time will take in more—the United States should feel free to invite individual countries to work with it if they so choose. The idea here is not to split Europe but rather to accept that at times it will be split—although probably not along lines that represent "old" and "new" Europe, as suggested by Secretary of Defense Donald Rumsfeld—and to work around it.

There will be no getting around the reality that the transatlantic relationship will not function in this era as it did during the Cold War without the cohesion induced by a widely shared perception of the Soviet threat. There is also the reality that almost all of the challenges to be met will be located outside Europe. This marks a significant change. Europe in the geographical sense was "a" and often "the" central battleground for much of the twentieth century. The fact that Europe today is almost entirely peaceful, democratic, and closely integrated economically means that for the foreseeable future, the fault lines of history will lie elsewhere. The strategic question is what Europeans are prepared to do outside Europe to influence this history. This change in geopolitical context along with the enlargement of both NATO and the EU almost certainly means that the alliance will act less as an alliance in the future. Instead, it is more realistic to expect selective partnerships developing between the United States and various collections of European countries, depending on the nature of the challenge at hand. The goal for the United States is the same, though, be it with clusters of European states or the EU: to work in harness, that is, to integrate them, in efforts to tame the challenges inherent in globalization and the post–Cold War world.

7

•

Integration and the Lessons of Iraq

INTEGRATION IS NOT and cannot be simply about policy. If it is to happen, it must also be about means, or process. It is useful to think about process in two ways: first, as the way by which major powers and others come to agree on what should be the organizing principles of contemporary international relations; and second, as the response made in specific instances when those principles are violated. No amount of prior consultation will guarantee consent and cooperation in specific circumstances. Blank checks are as rare in diplomacy as they are in other walks of life. Meaningful great power cooperation requires not simply agreement on principles but commitment to a process.

Organizing principles for any global endeavor require global participation and an attempt to forge consensus—in other words, diplomacy. Ideas need to be discussed in forums formal and informal, bilateral and multilateral, in public and in private. Consultation is the necessary prerequisite to negotiation. An important part, then, of integrating other countries is to involve them meaningfully in the process of establishing the rules and institutions meant to shape the world. Such consultation also provides an opportunity to persuade others of a particular point of view—and to decrease the chance for surprise when the principles are put to the test.

The State Department and the U.S. government more broadly spend too much time discussing immediate problems or negotiating specific agreements and too little in attempts to fashion creative structures and policies for dealing with how the world should be organized and international relations conducted. If there is consensus on why a form of intervention is acceptable in principle, there is a much greater chance that there will be explicit support for a particular intervention in practice. The absence of such consensus explains in part the breadth and depth of the falling out between the United States and much of the rest of the world over Iraq. There is also utility in simply making sure that other governments are aware of your concerns; such "signaling" can be a way to condition their behavior and to reduce the chance for surprise or miscalculation.

One approach to international process would be to require a central role for the UN Security Council. This is the preference of Russia, as made clear by its minister of defense: "[T]he United Nations alone can authorize the use of military force across internationally recognized borders. Any NATO action not approved by the United Nations should therefore be considered illegal—including 'preventive wars' like that in Iraq."[1] Under this approach, the major powers would agree not to act in important arenas of policy without Security Council approval or authorization. For example, there would be no humanitarian intervention or response to a state supporting terror or crossing some proliferation threshold unless the UN gave a green light.

There are, however, several substantial problems with this approach. The first pertains to the composition of the council, in both who is there and who is not. The UN Security Council represents what the Allies believed the world would look like in the aftermath of World War II. The council's composition was also based on subjective considerations as well as prediction. This explains why a much-weakened France was on the council—and both Germany and Japan were kept off it. India was still a British colony.

It would be impossible to make the case for the current composition of the Security Council—the five permanent members—if one were creating the institution today. Even counting China, members of the council represent under one-third of the world's peoples. No country from Latin America, Africa, the Middle East, or South Asia enjoys a permanent place on the fifteen-seat body. (The ten non-permanent seats are rotated among UN members.) More than 90 percent of the world's countries do not hold a seat at any given time. By contrast, Europe (with two permanent seats) is over-represented. Surely, Japan, India, Germany, possibly the EU, and others such as Brazil, Indonesia, and South Africa have strong cases for membership. Non-

state actors have no role. It is thus not surprising that con-
juring up alternative memberships for permanent members
is something of a cottage industry in both UN and academic circles. What these ideas tend to have in common is
expanding the size of the Security Council, either by adding
some new permanent members without a veto, by altering
the rotation so that certain countries get on the council
more often or for longer than two years, or some version of
both.[2]

All this activity notwithstanding, meaningful change is
unlikely to come about anytime soon. Remaking the council would inevitably help some countries and hurt others.
The two European members would resist being replaced
with a European seat; giving Germany a chair of its own
would only exacerbate the problem of Europe's overrepre-
sentation. Pakistan would object mightily to India, Ar-
gentina, Chile, and likewise, Mexico to Brazil, and Nigeria
to South Africa (or vice versa). The Middle East would
have its own problems, given rivalries among the Arab
states in addition to the questions of Iran and Israel; Asians
might agree to Japan but surely Indonesia (the world's
fourth most populous country) would want a seat, as would
South Korea, Australia, and no doubt others. All of which
raises the awkward question: How can a body that itself
lacks legitimacy in the eyes of many confer legitimacy?

But the problem of placing the Security Council at the
core of international relations and conflating legitimacy
with the United Nations in general and the Security Coun-

cil in particular goes beyond its composition. It is stranded on the lack of consensus among the five permanent members over what constitutes legitimate purpose in the world. The five confer nothing like the authority in the political-military realm to the UN that the WTO possesses over international trade. This was obvious in 2003 during the prelude to the Iraq war, when France, Russia, and possibly China were not prepared to support the United States and the United Kingdom. But it was no less obvious a few years earlier when neither China nor Russia was prepared to support the United States, Britain, and France by backing the intervention in Kosovo—or when the United States helped frustrate an international reaction to the unfolding tragedy in Rwanda. A lack of consensus would likely be evident if today the United States were to push for sanctions (not to mention military action) against North Korea or Iran or Sudan.

At the heart of the problem is the fact that no major power—not only the United States—accepts the right of another to veto a proposed course of action when it believes its vital national interests to be at stake. It is this absence of complete consensus and the Security Council's rules and composition that make it and the UN a too brittle and too narrow instrument to be the centerpiece of any attempt at this moment to build a more integrated world. This may change in the future, but we are not there now. We should not avoid the UN Security Council—when there is consensus, as there was after the Iraqi invasion of

Kuwait in 1990 or in the aftermath of 9/11, there is no better forum—but we cannot expect it to be the sole source of legitimacy in the world.

Many will disagree with this view. Less powerful governments tend to be more preoccupied with process, as it offers a means for them to have greater influence over what occurs in the world and to constrain the United States and other strong countries. But consider the case of Rwanda. If there had been an outside intervention to prevent the genocide, hundreds of thousands of innocent lives would have been spared. It would have been the right thing to do. It would have been legitimate because of what it was, not because it was approved by the UN. This is why the UN Report of the International Commission on Intervention and State Sovereignty commissioned by Secretary-General Kofi Annan several years ago goes too far. Acknowledging that situations such as Rwanda may arise when the UN fails to act even though it should, the report goes on to say, "It is a real question in these circumstances where lies the most harm: in the damage to international order if the Security Council is bypassed or in the damage to that order if human beings are slaughtered while the Security Council stands by."[3] But it should not be a real question. It is clearly wrong to confuse or equate the UN Security Council with legitimacy and to allow innocent people to perish for this principle.

The December 2004 report of the High-Level Panel appointed by Secretary-General Kofi Annan fell into the same trap of equating process (Security Council support) with legitimacy, in this case concerning preventive attacks.

The short answer is that if there are good arguments for preventive military action, with good evidence to support them, they should be put to the Security Council, which can authorize such action if it chooses to. If it does not so choose, there will be, by definition, time to pursue other strategies, including persuasion, negotiation, deterrence and containment—and to visit again the military option. For those impatient with such a response, the answer must be that, in a world full of perceived potential threats, the risk to global order and the norm of non-intervention on which it continues to be based is simply too great for the legality of unilateral preventive action, as distinct from collectively endorsed action, to be accepted. Allowing one to so act is to allow all.[4]

All the arguments have weight—but what will inevitably prevail is the instinct of any sovereign state not to cede such decisionmaking power to the United Nations and make its ability to act on behalf of what it sees as its vital interests dependent upon the support of others.

That seems to make for an impasse. But reality provides at least a partial way out. "Legitimacy" need not be understood as an absolute. It is as much about perception as it is a legal concept. It is also possible to be partly legitimate (or less than fully legitimate) and not be illegitimate. There ought to be a commitment by the United States and others to seek the broadest possible international agreement before undertaking an action, particularly one involving military force. The United Nations enjoys pride of place in the world of political-military issues. The United Nations matters if for no other reason than that many people around the world think it matters and because increasingly governments are constrained by what their people think. So it becomes worth the effort to have the UN Security Council endorse any contemplated action. If this appears or proves to be impossible, it need not be the end of the road. The United Nations is just one source of multilateralism. It is better to think of multilateralism as an à la carte phenomenon, not a single option, from which the choice includes the United Nations, NATO, a number of regional organizations, or the G-8. In principle, the G-8 could be transformed into an organization with a secretariat and more frequent meetings involving officials at various levels. Alternatively, it would be possible to create some new but expanded versions: a G-8 that would include several important countries not now members, that is, a G-10 with the addition of China and India. One could go further, and establish, say, a G-20 that would include the G-10 as well as such countries as Mexico, Brazil, Nigeria, South Africa, Indonesia, Pakistan, South Korea, Australia, Saudi Arabia, and Egypt. None of these, though, promises to be a panacea, as it is impossible to avoid questions of legitimacy over who would not be included and the problem of what to do when there is no consensus.

On the economic side, the most important players are the large international financial institutions—the IMF, the WTO, the World Bank—and informal groupings such as the G-7. The large organizations all have specific charters; that said, there are mounting calls for substantial change, especially in the IMF and World Bank.[5] There is also a growing consensus that the G-7 is inadequate, given the North Atlantic bias of the membership (Japan being the only exception). One could imagine any number of alternatives to the G-7. As in the political realm, there is the idea of an expanded version that would include China, India, and others (including a significant number of developing countries) in a G-20.[6] Or there are suggestions for a "shrunken" model along the lines of a G-4 steering group (consisting of the United States, the EU, Japan, and China), complemented by a council that would include fifteen countries as well as the leaders of the major international financial institutions and the UN.[7] Something along these lines is needed. The G-7, founded in 1978, is no longer adequate for the very different world that has evolved under globalization and the rise of Asia. Quite simply, too much of the world's population and too much of its economic activity are not represented.

Another alternative is to turn to or create more specialized international groupings consisting of those countries and others that are particularly relevant for a specific challenge. The six-power forum for North Korea (the United States, China, Japan, Russia, and both Koreas) is one such group, as is the "6 plus 2" (the United States, Russia, and Afghanistan's immediate neighbors) that played a constructive role in Afghanistan. So, too, is the "quartet" of the United States, Europe, Russia, and the United Nations that backs Middle East peace efforts. One could imagine similar groups for dealing with the Iran nuclear challenge (one effectively exists, involving several European governments, Russia, and the United States as well as the IAEA) or with a humanitarian crisis such as that in Darfur. These standing clusters (sometimes described as "contact groups") tend to gain in legitimacy and relevance if they include most or all the countries and other actors (be they NGOs, relevant international institutions, or corporations) needed to resolve the challenge at hand. They tend to be more effective if they are already in place. It gives them authority and the chance to prevent a crisis from materializing, or at least leaves them better positioned for dealing with it. Standing groups of this sort are more than so-called coalitions of the willing, which tend to be narrower in composition, reactive in nature, and as a result somewhat lacking in perceived legitimacy.

It can be argued, for example, that it was good and right that NATO provided the political as well as the military foundation for armed intervention in Kosovo when no consensus in the United Nations was forthcoming. Article 53 of the UN Charter actually got in the way: "[N]o enforcement action shall be taken under regional arrangements or by regional agencies without the authorization of the Security Council. . . ." It would be far better if designated regional organizations such as NATO did not require Security Council blessing beforehand; as we have seen in Rwanda and Darfur, such authorization may be slow in coming or never arrive at all, which can allow terrible situations to fester.

The need for a pragmatic case-by-case approach is evident. There must always be consideration given to the case for *not* acting in a particular context when no consensus among the major powers exists, given the long-term interest of encouraging the emergence of a world in which the major powers work at common and not cross purposes. There are some possible guidelines for navigating this unavoidable trade-off. It is important to give the process a fair chance and allow ample time for consensus to emerge at the UN Security Council. Consultations must be genuine and not simply an effort to insist on an already determined policy. A decision to opt out of formal multilateralism should only be made when there is an urgent need to act. The case must also be of sufficient weight or seriousness to justify acting. This is especially true when the intervention is military in nature. Preventive (as opposed to preemptive) uses of military force should remain a rare exception. Whenever a country elects to go its own way, it should go to great lengths to explain itself, in private as well as in public, with as many other governments in tow as possible. It is important that there be no unique benefit, such as special access to oil, contracts for firms, or military bases, that accrues to the United States or the country in question lest the intervention be seen as something other than one born of principle or necessity. And any country that decides to act without UN blessing should then return as soon as possible to the formal diplomatic fold, undertaking subsequent actions with the greatest possible global or regional involvement and authorization.

The reward to a country such as the United States if it follows such precepts should be that countries opposing the action in question would agree not to work actively against it. This willingness to tolerate or accept policies judged to be wrong or misguided is critical if integration or some version of a concert is to work. Countries cannot be expected to be passive if they judge their own vital national interests to be in danger; nor can they be expected to be silent if they disagree. But expecting that they would not actively oppose and work to frustrate one another's policies in lesser situations is a prerequisite for international cooperation to reach a higher level.

The Case of Iraq

THE RECENT CRISIS over Iraq is a valuable case study that illustrates the difficulties of translating these themes into policy. The United States acted inconsistently with these guidelines both before and after the Iraq war. This was not because, as many contended at the time and subsequently, the United States rushed UN Security Council consideration of the matter in early 2003. It is not at all clear that more time would have generated much of an international consensus to act; to the contrary, it is more likely that the continued inability of inspectors to find weapons of mass destruction (as we now know would have been the case) would have led more governments to conclude that there were no weapons and argue that there was no reason for the United States to resort to force. The counterargument put forward by the U.S. and British governments, that inspections could not be expected to turn up weapons because Iraq had not provided the United Nations with the required accounting of its weapons programs and relevant imports, had the advantages of legality and logic but for most people and governments did not rise to the level of justifying a war. Making the case for preventive war requires some proof of the positive that the problem exists; not being able to prove the negative, that a country does not possess nuclear weapons, is unlikely to be enough to convince many other states to support a preventive use of military force.

In such situations, the United States or any country has four options. It can take an issue to the UN Security Council, gain support, and act. This was what happened in the 1990–1991 Gulf crisis in the aftermath of Iraq's invasion of Kuwait. It can elect not to go to the council and act either unilaterally or with some other standing or ad hoc grouping. This is reminiscent of the U.S. intervention in Grenada in 1983. It can go to the council, discover that it does not have adequate support, avoid a formal vote that it would lose, and act. This was what the United States did in early 2003 in the Iraq case when it became clear no second resolution specifically authorizing the use of military force against Iraq would be forthcoming from the Security Council and what the United States, France, and the United Kingdom did a few years before at the time of the Kosovo crisis. A fourth option is to take an issue to the UN, lose, but go ahead and act regardless. This last course was considered by the Bush administration during the Iraq crisis in early 2003 but was wisely rejected on the grounds that it would cause more international outcry and opposition than acting without a new and explicit UN mandate.

It is impossible to discuss these alternatives and not get into a debate about legality and legitimacy. Legality is a narrow, technical term, one that reflects whether a nation is acting in conformity with the law and, in this context, with the letter of the UN Charter. Legitimacy is a broader term, one that is inherently more subjective and that considers matters of context, intent, and means. It can be argued, for example, that the Kosovo decision lacked legality (in that it bypassed the Security Council) but that it enjoyed considerable legitimacy. It was approved by a relevant regional organization and was motivated by a dire humanitarian crisis; further, no other option was available, and those using military force did not do so out of a narrow self-interest. By contrast, what the United States and the United Kingdom did in Iraq in 2003 was legal, or in any event was surely closer to being legal than the Kosovo operation in that Iraq had by then violated more than a dozen Security Council dictates, including Resolution 687, which set the terms of the post–Gulf War cease-fire, and Resolution 1441, which demanded that Iraq give complete cooperation to the UN weapons inspectors or face serious consequences. But whether it was legitimate is an open question. The reality that it was widely perceived not to be legitimate had real consequences for the United States, including a dramatic reduction in the scale of international support that was forthcoming and a no less dramatic rise in the level of anti-Americanism around the world. What is not known is how much this action might complicate getting other powers to work with the United States when future contingencies arise—and to what extent it might contribute to their using military force on occasions in the future when the United States would prefer that they did not.

In the end, though, the problem with U.S. policy toward Iraq had less to do with Security Council tactics than with the fundamental decision that the status quo was intolerable and that preventive war was a necessary course of action. When it came to nuclear weapons, the intelligence at the time did not support acting. Iraq did not possess nuclear weapons or even a nuclear weapons program worthy of the name. Nor was it inevitable that over time Iraq would have been able to develop nuclear weapons, given the international sanctions in place. And if it did, there was always the possibility of acting in a preventive or preemptive mode if intelligence showed Iraq somehow was developing nuclear weapons—something it would have had great difficulty in hiding under the circumstances—or was preparing to use them.

The other and stronger argument for preventive war against Saddam's Iraq rested on chemical and biological weapons. The presumption at the time the decision was made to go to war was that Saddam possessed both chemical and biological weapons. This was the prevailing interpretation of his refusal to comply fully with various UN Security Council resolutions requiring that he both provide a full accounting of any materials or technologies in Iraq's possession relating to weapons of mass destruction and cooperate fully with international inspectors. Alternative explanations, including a desire to deter others (most notably Iran) from attacking Iraq out of fear he might use WMD or a wish not to lose face, were given little credence at the time, although in retrospect it appears that they were closer to the truth. There was understandable concern that Saddam might use chemical or biological weapons against his own people or his neighbors, two things he had done in the past. A more serious concern after 9/11 was that Saddam might transfer these weapons or capabilities to terrorists. Still, this would have been uncharacteristic, in light of Iraq's mostly lapsed ties to terrorists and Saddam's penchant for control. And had such a transfer been shown to have taken place, the United States would have been in a far stronger position to garner international support for action akin to what it did to the Taliban in Afghanistan following 9/11.

It was also possible that Saddam could transfer biological and chemical agents he was thought to possess to terrorists without the knowledge of the United States and the world. There was therefore a hypothetical risk in not acting preventively. Reasonable, thoughtful people could and did differ on the significance of this risk and the importance of acting in order to prevent it from happening. But the lion's share of the argument for acting preventively depended on Saddam's actually possessing chemical and biological weapons. The case for acting in a preventive mode is simply not there otherwise, which is why the intelligence failure is so important and why good intelligence is so central to the argument for preventive war.

Other rationales for the Iraq war were even weaker. It is true that Saddam was a major abuser of human rights. But the moment for a massive humanitarian intervention was in 1988, when he used chemical munitions against the Kurds. Also, subsequently, the international community created no-fly zones pursuant to Security Council Resolution 688 so that the U.S.-led Gulf War coalition could better monitor Saddam's actions and take steps to protect the Iraqi people. The human rights situation in Iraq in 2002 did not warrant armed intervention. Links between Iraq and al Qaeda (and terrorists more generally) were marginal. There was no evidence tying Iraq or Saddam to the 9/11 attacks.

Going to war to bring democracy to Iraq (and through Iraq to the region), no matter how laudable a goal, simply does not constitute a valid rationale, given the human and financial costs of doing so, the uncertain prospects for success, the availability of alternative tools to promote democratic change, and the dangerous precedent it sets for international relations. We do not want to make it acceptable to use force for such purposes, lest we bring back a world in which the use of military force becomes commonplace.

The alternative to going to war in 2002 was not inaction but continuing to rely on sanctions as the centerpiece of U.S. and international policy. As we now know, sanctions, introduced in the aftermath of Iraq's 1990 invasion of Kuwait, were working fairly well in denying Iraq the ability to reconstitute its weapons of mass destruction. What is more, they could have worked far better. The administration of George W. Bush made sanctions "smarter" only in the sense of allowing Iraq to import a wider range of consumer goods, thereby removing the bogus but politically effective argument that sanctions were hurting innocent Iraqi people. The sanctions could and should have been made smarter in another sense, namely, in shutting down Iraq's illegal trade (mostly oil in exchange for dollars that Saddam used to maintain domestic political support and purchase items on the black market) with Iraq's neighbors. The United States could have subsidized the Turkish and Jordanian economies—that would have cost approximately $500 million a year, cheap compared to the cost of war—in exchange for their curtailing most of their illicit trade with Iraq. Conventional military force or possibly covert action could have been used to shut down the Iraq-Syria oil pipeline that was a source to Saddam Hussein of significant revenue (nearly $3 billion over twelve years) outside international control. We now know that 84 percent of the hard currency that illegally reached Saddam Hussein during the years that the sanctions were in effect (1991–2003) did so via trade arrangements with Jordan, Syria, Turkey, and Egypt or because of smuggling; only 16 percent was the result of kickbacks and other abuses of the UN-run "oil for food" program, under which Iraq could legally sell oil and import a wide range of goods.[8]

If the United States had stuck with sanctions and eschewed war, Saddam would almost certainly still be in power today. Many have posed the question as to whether Iraq and the world are better off without Saddam Hussein. It is and we are, but this is not a terribly useful question. It would be akin in a business setting to looking only at revenues and ignoring expenses. What matters in business as well as in foreign policy is the balance or relationship between costs and benefits. It is this assessment that leads to the judgment that the war against Iraq was unwarranted. The direct costs to the United States, at the time of this writing—1,500 American soldiers killed; more than 10,000 who have sustained serious injury; the $200-billion tab; the absorption of a high percentage of U.S. military might—were and are simply too high, given what was at stake. The

U.S. effort in Iraq absorbed resources that could have better been used elsewhere and placed additional pressures on the already strained economic and military foundations of American power. Senior officials in government devoted an enormous amount of their time and energy to Iraq. More serious and immediate challenges to U.S. well-being, including the nuclear challenges posed by Iran and North Korea, the stabilization of Afghanistan, the effort to promote peace between Israelis and Palestinians, and relations with the other major powers, did not get the attention they deserved.[9] Other tools and policies were available to foster political and economic change throughout the Arab world; the war against Iraq was necessary only to bring immediate political change to Iraq.

Launching a preventive war when it was not warranted works directly against the ability of the United States to develop and benefit from the opportunity that exists to bring about a world in which other major powers will work with the United States to promote common objectives. It lowers the bar that discourages such attacks by other countries against states they view to be dangerous. It alienates governments and publics from the United States, making cooperation in other areas more difficult. And a costly experience in Iraq could also stimulate greater domestic opposition in the United States to an active U.S. world role as citizens grow to increasingly question the costs of a foreign policy informed more by choice than necessity. As Hans Morgenthau has written, "Good motives give assurance against deliberately bad policies; they do not guarantee the moral goodness and political success of the policies they inspire."[10]

The United States did not do much better in the war's aftermath. Any largely unilateral action of the sort carried out by the United States against Iraq should be followed up as quickly as possible with a sincere attempt to get as many of the other major powers and as much of the international community as possible involved. By contrast, the Bush administration was slow to involve the United Nations and bring in others, resisting a new resolution that would have created a basis for substantial UN and international involvement in Iraq's political, economic, and physical reconstruction. Security Council Resolution 1546, which was approved in June 2004, could and should have been introduced and adopted more than a year earlier. In retrospect, the reasons for the delay are ironic and then some. There was the feeling in some quarters of the U.S. government that the United States had borne the brunt of the costs of the war and should not welcome to Iraq those who had not done their share or, worse yet, opposed the war. "To the victor should go the spoils" captures this thinking. This mindset was reinforced by the assessment (tragically wrong as it turned out) that the aftermath would be neither terribly difficult nor costly and that, as a result, the United States could succeed with little outside assistance. And there was a fear that control over the aftermath (and with it, decisive influence over which Iraqis would assume power) would be forfeited if the UN assumed a leading position inside Iraq. "Once the international bureaucrats get their hands on a society, they never let go," is how David Frum and Richard Perle put it.[11]

The decision to delay giving the United Nations and others a meaningful role in the aftermath was misguided. The opportunity to heal diplomatic rifts was squandered. So, too, was the chance to get others to assume a substantial portion of the military and financial burden of stabilizing and rebuilding Iraq. The international presence quickly came to be viewed by many Iraqis as an American occupation. A policy of integration, if it is to have any chance of succeeding, requires broadening international participation in important undertakings, even at the price of some loss of autonomy and freedom of action. It was in the interests of the United States to have made such a trade-off in the Iraq case, much as it would have made sense to give Europeans and others a meaningful role in the operation to liberate Afghanistan.

But it would also have been worthwhile for others to meet the United States halfway. This is where France and other governments deserve their share of criticism. As noted earlier, a doctrine of integration and efforts to construct a rudimentary international concert will only advance if those who disagree with a given policy forgo the option of actively opposing it. By this measure, France should have argued in private for a different policy, and even criticized the policy openly, but it should not have threatened to veto it.

None of this changes the importance that the United States and the coalition (and the international community more broadly) succeed in Iraq. Success means establishing a functioning country with some degree of political rights and enough stability so that essential political and economic life can take place safely. Iraq need not be a democratic paragon. But any outcome that involved the United States being perceived to be run out of Iraq by terrorists (as opposed to being asked to leave by an elected Iraqi government) would be a foreign policy debacle, not just for the United States but for all the major powers and for the world. It would set back the prospects for the opportunity that is at the core of this book. In addition to the immediate human, economic, and strategic costs in Iraq, such an outcome would encourage terrorist and radical groups elsewhere in the region and undermine the morale and stability of relatively moderate regimes overseeing countries with the potential to evolve into fairly open political and economic entities and which in some cases control key resources. The domino effect may have been overstated in Southeast Asia a generation ago, but it could well apply here. At some point, investment and involvement create their own national security stakes; for better or worse, this is now the case in Iraq.

Iraq has also proved that it is not enough to have a military that can fight modern wars. It is also essential to have a military that can consolidate peace. The latter mission is not less demanding so much as different. It cannot be assumed that forces trained and equipped to handle all-out combat can inherently handle situations involving nontraditional forms of hostilities in urban environments. More troops with different training and tactics and equipment are needed for what the Pentagon has traditionally defined as involving "military operations other than wars," that is, operations better understood as "peacemaking," not "peacekeeping."[12] This mission will require additional financial resources and possibly dedicated forces.[13] It is also a mission that could naturally be shared with forces from Europe and elsewhere in conjunction with a regional organization, the United Nations, or a less formal coalition of the able and willing. Such cooperation would constitute yet another significant example of integration at work.

8

•

The Necessity

THIS BOOK is titled *The Opportunity* because the underlying characteristics of our era—principally the fact that conflict between or among the major powers of today is remote, a development that frees China, Russia, Japan, India, and the countries of Europe to work with the United States to tackle common challenges—are uncommonly benign. They offer the possibility to restructure international relations in a qualitatively different, positive, and lasting way.

This book could just have easily been titled "The Necessity." The principal challenges of this era—the spread of weapons of mass destruction and nuclear weapons in particular, terrorism, renewed protectionism, infectious disease, drugs, climate change—must be met collectively or they will come to overwhelm the United States and the other major powers and define the era.

Either way, opportunity or necessity, what we know is that global order will not come about on its own. History suggests just the opposite: Without concerted effort by the major powers of the day, the world will degenerate into warring factions in which liberty and prosperity are early victims. The U.S. role is critical. Only U.S. leadership has the potential to be forceful and generous enough to persuade the other major powers to come together and build a more integrated world that can take on challenges to the common peace and prosperity.

The United States will need to adjust its foreign policy to cooperate more with other countries if we are to avoid a return to the classic balance-of-power politics that would drain valuable resources that ought to be devoted elsewhere. That is why the goal of integrating the major powers of the day into international efforts and arrangements designed to combat the dangerous dimensions of globalization is so vital. Enlisting others in a narrow campaign against terrorists and those who support them will simply be insufficient in light of the range of challenges confronting the United States and the rest of the world.

Integration cannot be limited to the major powers, as important as they are for the future. It needs to include those medium powers such as Brazil, South Africa, Nigeria, South Korea, Australia, Indonesia, and others, all of whom exert considerable influence in their respective regions and on occasion beyond. A concerted effort must also be made to integrate those who have largely missed out on the benign aspects of modernity and whose lives are circumscribed by poverty. Half of this problem will be addressed if China and India sustain their high-growth paths. The others, though, will need a mix of assistance conditioned on the adoption of proven economic and political reforms, aid to combat disease, and the elimination of trade measures that limit or block access to the markets of the wealthy countries. It is right in a humanitarian sense, and right with regard to global security, to prevent states from failing or to help rescue those who do, so that they do not become exporters of conflict and terror.

Implicit in all this are two realities. First, there is no way the United States can protect itself and promote its interests if it pulls back from the world. Isolationism is an anachronism in a global era.

The second truth is that for all of its power, there is virtually nothing the United States can do better without others. The United States needs partners; unilateralism is rarely a viable option. The United States cannot, for example, go to war without access to the bases and airspace of others. To stop terrorism the United States needs other governments to share intelligence and to make their law enforcement agencies available. The United States alone cannot ensure that the technologies and materials needed to make nuclear weapons or the explosive material that is their chief component do not get into the wrong hands.

For all America's wealth and might, it cannot readily rebuild Afghanistan, Iraq, and other needy states without widespread participation by other governments and the United Nations. U.S. authorities cannot keep their citizens safe from SARS and HIV/AIDS without the cooperation of other public health agencies. Taking meaningful steps to slow global climate change will require global participation. The flows of goods, services, and capital that fuel the American economy and standard of living are in part generated by other governments, organizations, and firms. Sanctions only bite if they are imposed by virtually everyone. As a result, the real foreign policy debate ought not to be whether to choose unilateralism or multilateralism, but rather how to choose wisely among the various forms of the latter, that is, when to turn to the UN as opposed to other standing clusters of states, alliances, regional groupings, contact groups, or ad hoc coalitions of the willing. The guiding principle should be to aim for forms of cooperation that are as broad and as formal as possible—and to choose narrow (less inclusive) and informal forms of cooperation only as required.

The ability to get others to work with the United States will depend mostly on persuading them of the merits of the policies under consideration. As was once said in another setting, however, foreign policy is not social work, and Americans cannot expect other governments to support the United States out of charity or goodwill. A number of factors will affect the behavior of other governments when it comes to associating themselves with U.S. leadership, including the extent to which the United States is responsive to their concerns when their vital interests are in play. U.S. officials can never forget that foreign policy is forged in a context and that all relationships (even between unequals) must be reciprocal.

The responsibility for realizing the opportunity cannot fall on American shoulders alone. To be sure, a good deal of this book has been written for Americans and directed at the current and future governments of the United States. But on its own, the United States cannot succeed in making the world safer or more prosperous or more just. It needs partners, which it must recognize, but its would-be partners must also recognize this equally. This means being both able and willing to act, at times militarily, at times diplomatically or economically, in a manner that makes promoting order more important than realizing immediate profit or popularity. It also means forgoing the temptation to actively work against a fellow major power except in those rare instances when truly vital national interests are at play.

How the United States conducts its foreign policy also counts for a great deal. The United States is not the only country with domestic opinion that influences and constrains policy choices. Diplomacy need not be a dirty word. Tone matters. The U.S. government should avoid just saying "no" and instead put forward a serious alternative when some proposed international arrangement such as the Kyoto Protocol or the International Criminal Court is judged to be unacceptable. The United States must also be careful to act consistently with its own stated objectives; it is difficult to be a credible spokesman for open trade if at the same time the United States maintains subsidies or unfairly protects its own manufacturers from foreign competition. Acting consistently with principle is no less important; the sort of abuses that went on at the Abu Ghraib prison undermine the ability of the United States to be an effective advocate in the world for human rights and respect for the rule of law.

Consultations need to be frequent and genuine and address the big issues of the era, including when the use of military force is warranted; what should be done when states with a history of aggression and support for terrorism set out to acquire weapons of mass destruction; what can be done to make the United Nations more effective and what courses of action are acceptable when the organization is deadlocked; what should be determined as the obligations of sovereignty; and what can and should be done when a government fails to meet its obligations either to its own citizens or to the world. It is too late to raise such questions in the middle of a crisis. Fundamental discussions about legitimate uses of force and how the world is to be organized more broadly should not be put off.

What others think of the United States and U.S. foreign policy also matters. Anti-Americanism is anything but cost free. In the short run, it affects how much cooperation and burden sharing can be generated. This is critical for two reasons. Most global issues require global responses. And going it alone will prove not only ineffective but expensive and, over time, will erode the foundations of American strength that in part account for the existence of the opportunity. There is also a long-term price to be paid for anti-American attitudes, as people who come of age hating the United States will one day come to power mistrustful of the United States, or worse. This will only make future efforts to organize collective responses to common problems more difficult.

The United States requires a full range of foreign policy tools. Modern military forces are needed to discourage wars and to prevail if they come about all the same. But the forces and equipment that are needed on battlefields do not easily, much less automatically, make the transition to the sort of messy post-conflict situations that increasingly characterize today's world. The United States cannot ultimately succeed in the world by relying on military force. The words of Otto von Bismarck come to mind: "You can do everything with bayonets, but you are not able to sit on them." Military force is irrelevant when dealing with disease or global climate change or protectionism or massive poverty or striking inequality. Instead, the most relevant tools in some situations tend to be diplomacy, foreign assistance, trade and investment flows, and the provision of education and training. Intelligence gathering and sharing is likely to be the most valuable instrument in combating today's terrorism; educational and economic reform may prove to be the most valuable in discouraging tomorrow's. In most instances, military force can be no more effective than the information that guides it. Moreover, military force is expensive in both human and dollar terms—certainly more so than diplomacy. A principal foreign policy challenge is to prevent problems from reaching the stage where a military response is all that remains.

A degree of modesty is also called for. The answer to problems caused by a particular government will rarely be to demand that the government be removed. Regime change tends to be difficult and, if it involves defeating and occupying the country in question, costly by every measure. It cannot be counted on to bring about a desired effect in the short run. This means that other policies, normally involving putting forward a package of incentives and penalties linked to specific changes in behavior, will almost always be required to influence the behavior of difficult or dangerous governments. Integration of both the "target" country and of other countries in the effort to shape its policies is likely to be more successful.

It is essential not to lose sight of priorities. The promotion of democracy and human rights is both good and necessary, but it is rarely something that can be allowed to crowd out other objectives. This is especially the case when it comes to countries such as China, Russia, and Pakistan, where the priority must lie with combating the spread of weapons of mass destruction and terrorism. Nor can the Middle East afford to wait for democracy before it can achieve peace. Democracy should be promoted, but it cannot always take precedent—and even when it does, the promotion of democracy can often best be achieved by encouraging economic reform and drafting of constitutions rather than the show of elections.

This is a time for new, creative thinking that embraces other powers as partners more than rivals. New international institutions and arrangements are needed to address specific challenges; new forms of economic governance are needed to regulate relationships among currencies. New arrangements are also called for in the Western Hemisphere, including ones that would bring about a more integrated North American "community" better able to promote economic growth and deal with security, environmental, energy, and labor challenges. Governments can no longer be allowed to hide behind sovereignty and abuse their own people. If and when they do, the international community has a right and an obligation to act to protect the innocent. Governments that support terrorism or transfer or use weapons of mass destruction similarly forfeit the advantages of sovereignty and again open themselves up to international sanction, including their removal.

Fresh thinking about sovereignty is not the only relevant feature of a foreign policy that concerns itself with internal developments elsewhere. Clearly, what happens "over there" can affect what happens here. On occasion this can require outside involvement with such matters as educational, political, and economic reform. We need to absorb the idea that the failure of other countries to provide political and economic opportunity to their citizens is not just a humanitarian or moral problem but a strategic one as well, as such societies all too often spawn radicals and terrorists.

Success in the world will also require that the United

States act to put its own house in order. A number of things come to mind here, including reducing the fiscal deficit that will over time draw away resources available for overseas commitments. This will likely require some mixture of tax increases and, arguably more important, a reduction in the growth of federal spending, which in turn will require entitlement reform. A policy of guns, butter, and lower taxes is not sustainable. The U.S. government also needs to put into place policies that encourage saving. Just as essential is cutting the energy consumption that distorts American foreign policy, weakens the dollar, and contributes to global climate change. Improving the quality of education and adopting policies that encourage lifelong learning and sustained research will also help Americans compete in a global marketplace and build public support for policies that embrace globalization rather than fight it. Such reform at home will have another dividend, namely, that American efforts to persuade others to put their domestic houses in order are likely to be far more successful if the United States itself is widely viewed as a model, one that practices what it preaches.

There is some urgency to all this. The opportunity that now exists is not permanent. It will over time fade or even disappear altogether. The world may be on the brink of a tipping point in the decades-long battle to prevent the spread of weapons of mass destruction. Terrorists are increasing in number, and at the same time they are certainly increasing in sophistication and the ability to cause great harm. Anti-Americanism, which makes it harder to persuade others to share burdens now and could over time bring to positions of power leaders whose world outlook is informed by a suspicion of American power, risks becoming pervasive and permanent. The economic strength that is the foundation for all the United States does in the world is in jeopardy, given the large gap between what the U.S. government spends and takes in. The U.S. economy is vulnerable to the swings of currency markets, a loss of access to adequate supplies of oil and gas, or both. The fate of current trade negotiations could have an enormous impact on world economic growth.

The result is that opportunity coexists with necessity and urgency. It is not inevitable that things turn out right. This could easily become an era akin to the last one, defined by cold war, or even worse, defined by chaos. But just as easily, this could still turn out to be an era of great promise, one defined by lasting peace, improving standards of living, and greater freedom. There is little in the way of resource limits or institutional barriers to prevent the United States from choosing such a course. Future generations will have grounds to be critical and then some if it turns out that we failed to seize the opportunity at hand.

EPILOGUE

T HE PREMISE OF *The Opportunity* is straightforward: we live in a rare age in which prospects for great power conflict are remote, a state of affairs that shields the United States, China, Japan, Russia, Europe, and India from the devastating costs of major war and offers the hope that these countries can increasingly cooperate to meet the pressing regional and global challenges of the day.

The United States can make the most of this opportunity, one that can be viewed as a respite from history, only by adopting a foreign policy founded on a doctrine of integration. Integration requires a commitment to bringing in other powers as partners to work together on behalf of common goals; establishing new international rules and organizations most governments are willing to abide by; lifting hundreds of millions out of poverty and into modernity through trade, investment, and the provision of aid linked to economic and political reforms; working to persuade and pressure rogue regimes to revise their ways;

and doing everything possible to help young Arabs and Muslims become fully part of the societies in which they live, be they in the Middle East and Asia or in Western Europe and North America.

The foreign policy of the first term of President George W. Bush was largely inconsistent with these principles. There are, however, elements of policy change (viewed here as progress) to report in some realms and in some places. Thanks to expanded production and sharing of intelligence, law enforcement cooperation, and homeland security efforts in the United States and elsewhere, it is now more difficult for terrorists to succeed in many parts of the world. In September 2005, the United States joined with China, Japan, Russia, and both South and North Korea to announce a package of economic, political, and energy-related incentives tied to North Korea abandoning nuclear weapons and associated programs and reentering the nonproliferation regime. Months later, and following intense consultations, the United States joined with the EU, China, and Russia to fashion a package of incentives and penalties designed to roll back Iran's developing nuclear capabilities. The United States provided much of the impetus for the negotiation of a peace accord in the Darfur region of Sudan in an attempt to halt genocide there. U.S.-India ties potentially reached a new level with the signing of an accord to facilitate nuclear cooperation between the two countries and to give momentum to the bilateral relationship. And the U.S. government spoke of its goal of persuading China to become a "stakeholder," in other words, a country deeply integrated into efforts to promote order in Asia and around the world.

What accounts for this partial shift? There appears to be greater acceptance within the current U.S. administration that a foreign policy shaped by integration (regardless of whether it is so described) is essential to protecting U.S. interests in the contemporary world. Today's principal challenges— the spread of nuclear weapons, terrorism, protectionism— are manifestations of globalization that do not lend themselves to being solved by any single country. Collective, coordinated, or common action is required lest the problems overwhelm the United States and everyone else.

In fact, the United States has had little choice but to embrace integration. There is more than a little irony at work in this, as it was Iraq—a country with which we have engaged in a classic war of choice that in both design and execution rejected many of the premises of integration— that has limited the unilateral and military options available to the United States. The United States is paying a steep price for the ill-conceived and even more poorly implemented policy of transformation in Iraq. As of this writing, approximately 2,600 American military personnel have lost their lives; the financial costs are in the hundreds of billions of dollars and will be much higher once long-term medical expenses and the costs of replacing military equipment are factored in; the U.S. military is worse off, with new questions about its ability to recruit and retain the best personnel; the United States has forfeited leverage vis-à-vis Iran, the biggest strategic benefactor of Iraq's weakening and the rise of the Shia within Iraq; a new generation of terrorists schooled on the streets of Baghdad has emerged; and we are seeing greater anti-Americanism in a critical region and beyond. As a result, the gap between America's capacities and the challenges arrayed against these capacities has grown so large as to require a more multilateral approach to foreign policy.

Moreover, the partial embrace of integration in certain instances should not obscure where progress has not materialized. It is one thing to announce an approach to deal with a North Korean or Iranian nuclear challenge, something quite different (and more difficult) to implement it. In the case of North Korea, the agreement is a paper one; little has been done to eliminate North Korea's stockpile of nuclear material and possibly weapons. China in particular appears unwilling to use all of its leverage lest it trigger North Korea's collapse, something that could lead to large refugee flows into China and the emergence of a united Korea closely associated with the United States.

There is widespread opposition to Iran producing weapons-grade uranium and developing nuclear weapons. But this does not ensure that the major powers will be able to deal with Iran from a position of relative strength, i.e., with a united front. Differences will inevitably emerge when it comes to defining what lesser steps by Iran might be tolerable in the realm of nuclear research and enrichment—or what sanctions to introduce should Iran reject such limits.

Differences are not limited to the nonproliferation realm. It is not at all apparent that objections to the continuing genocide in Sudan will lead to a commitment to meaningful sanctions, much less adequate military force to protect those who are vulnerable. Chances for agreement on a new global trade round are slim, despite the fact that failure to reach an accord would do more to slow down the integration of the world's poor than any amount of aid can offset. And international efforts to do something meaningful about slowing climate change remain meager. Worse, there is little evidence that consensus is emerging about what to do when the Kyoto Protocol expires in 2012.

A number of explanations account for the fact that today's world can be characterized as one of, at best, limited integration. These explanations go beyond the basic reality that other governments pursue what they see as their self-interest and that there is, and always will be, disagreement among the major powers of any era over the means and ends of international relations. One significant explanation, however, is to be found in American foreign policy. There is still more than a little aversion to multilateral cooperation out of the concern that it limits U.S. freedom of action. There is also a persistent strand of anti-globalization that manifests itself as protectionism, be it of the trade or investment sort. And there remains a reluctance to embrace diplomacy, a tendency manifested by the opposition to bilateral negotiations with North Korea, to comprehensive, unconditional negotiations with Iran, to a meaningful dialogue with Syria, and to putting forward the outlines of a final settlement between Israel and the Palestinians. This reluctance reflects a misunderstanding of diplomacy, which at its core is not a favor or reward for others but simply one instrument to be employed on those occasions it has the potential to promote the national interest.

Above all, there is an emphasis of debatable wisdom in American foreign policy on promoting democratic change. At its core, a foreign policy premised on promoting "freedom" is a reflection of the democratic peace argument, which contends that history shows mature democracies treat their own citizens and their neighbors relatively benignly. The argument asserts that meaningful global integration is best achieved by democratic transformation.

The problems with this approach to foreign policy are less philosophical than practical. Mature democracies are more peaceful. But creating mature democracies is no easy task. To the contrary, it is difficult to think of anything more daunting. It is by definition impossible to create a mature democracy instantly or even quickly. Pacing, the sequencing of political and economic reform, taking into account local culture and tradition—these and other factors complicate all efforts to instill (much less install) democratic ways. Partial successes can translate into total failures, as incomplete or "emerging" democracies are prone to populism and extreme nationalism. Elections, far from being a panacea, can introduce additional problems. In Iraq, they have reinforced sectarian rather than national identity; in Palestine, elections have brought to power a party with an agenda inconsistent with conflict resolution.

What is more, all of this social engineering necessarily takes place at the same time the United States must call upon some of the very governments it seeks to change (and, on occasion, oust) to join with it to meet the pressing political, economic, and strategic challenges of the day. Emphasizing the need for dramatic political reform can make cooperation on other priority matters more difficult; backing off opens the United States to charges of hypocrisy and double standards.

For these reasons, the principal business of American foreign policy must be the foreign policy, not the domestic policy, of others. This certainly applies to dealings with major nondemocratic powers such as China and Russia, whose cooperation is essential to meet such challenges as the spread of nuclear weapons. But it also applies to rogue states such as North Korea and Iran. The United States does not have the luxury of hoping that regime change will come soon enough to persuade these countries to forsake terror or render their possession of nuclear weapons less troublesome. This argues for working to integrate them now despite their significant domestic flaws.

This is not to argue for a narrowly "realist," much less amoral, foreign policy. To the contrary, there are humanitarian and practical reasons alike to favor more open societies.

But promoting internal reform is only one goal among many, and rarely can or should it dominate. There is also the question of how to go about promoting reform. Here, too, integration makes sense, as it has the potential to do more to foster internal evolution than sanctioning and isolation, policies that seem mostly to retard the emergence of a private sector and middle class (often the best engines of democracy) while strengthening the hands of leaders who blame the United States for the failures of their own governments.

Iraq is perhaps the ultimate example where a foreign policy of transformation proved distorting. This is not to deny the dividends of the American-inspired and -led effort in Iraq—Saddam today stands trial, no longer in a position to threaten his own people or his neighbors, Iraqis have enjoyed the chance to vote for multiple governments and a constitution—but simply to point out that the current and projected costs of recent Iraq policy are greater than any current or reasonably projected benefits and that the net impact has had profound consequences for U.S. national security elsewhere. Hopes that regime change in Iraq would lead to a broader political transformation of the region appear unfounded. The opposite appears more likely to be true: events in Iraq have disillusioned many in the Arab world about democracy given the violence and the loss of Sunni political primacy. Iraq is likely to be a messy and somewhat dysfunctional country for years or even decades to come; at worst, it could become a failed state characterized by civil conflict that invariably draws in several of its neighbors. It is increasingly clear that the war in Iraq, a war of choice, was a bad choice.

Hopes for near-term transformation have undermined U.S. policy elsewhere; indeed, valuable years were lost while the United States distracted itself with fanciful hopes of regime change. Lost time allowed North Korea to expand its nuclear arsenal. It also allowed Iran to continue clandestine efforts to develop an enrichment capability. In the process, the United States squandered the chance to pressure Iran when oil was one-third its current price, before the United States became bogged down in Iraq, and when Iran was governed by someone more open to normal relations with the outside world. The good news is that there is evidence that the United States is finally coming to the realization, however belatedly and haltingly, that a policy predicated on achieving regime change any time soon in either North Korea or Iran is more wish than strategy. American foreign policy needs to be rethought: a foreign policy premised on promoting integration is more likely over time to achieve democratic transformation than is a policy that sees democratic transformation as a means to achieve integration and its dividends.

But it is not simply what the United States is doing abroad that jeopardizes prospects for bringing about a more integrated and successful world. It is also what the United States is *not* doing at home. There is little that suggests the United States is prepared to deal with the internal challenges to its continued capacity to act effectively (and discourage challenge) abroad. Neither the executive branch nor Congress demonstrates a willingness to cut domestic spending or selectively raise taxes, while restoring American competitiveness will require years of concerted but hard-to-bring-about action, including K–12 educational reform and a selective easing of immigration limits.

Most pressing is American energy dependence. The president's statement in his 2006 State of the Union, that "America is addicted to oil, which is often imported from unstable parts of the world," is true. Unfortunately, the policies put forward by the administration fail to match the scale of the problem. The current state of affairs is extremely costly: in terms of dollar flows (many of which go to leaders and countries pursuing aims inimical to the United States); in terms of increasing the burdens of the world's poor; in terms of exacerbating factors bringing about climate change. The solution lies in some mixture of near and mid-term policies designed to hasten the emergence of alternatives to oil and gas and in reducing the amount of oil and gas consumed. This translates into higher gasoline taxes (offset by reductions in income or payroll taxes) and higher fuel economy requirements for cars and light trucks, and it would also require a range of incentives to speed the introduction of alternatives. Unfortunately, gaining sufficient political support for such steps is a long-shot at best.

One year after it first appeared I would still title this book *The Opportunity* if I were publishing it for the first time. That said, it would be less than candid of me if I did not acknowledge that the prospects for the opportunity to become reality are less than they were. This is a sobering conclusion; anyone wondering what the alternative to an integrated world could or would look like need look no further than the Middle East, which as of this writing resembles an unstable and often violent cauldron of competing local states, terrorist groups, failed and failing countries, and sectarian violence with outside powers possessing only a limited capacity to order regional developments. It is not too late to reverse such trends, but fostering improvement will be difficult and success is anything but inevitable. To the contrary, change for the better in the Middle East and beyond will require concerted change in U.S. foreign and domestic policy alike.

RICHARD N. HAASS,

August 2006

Acknowledgments

THIS BOOK ONLY came to see the light of day because of the support of others. I want to begin by going back some thirty years, to several of my professors at Oxford. There I was fortunate to work with Albert Hourani, Alastair Buchan, Michael Howard, and Hedley Bull. Because of them, I first began to think systematically about American foreign policy and international relations. In important ways, this book is the long-delayed product of their collective efforts.

I also want to acknowledge my former colleagues on the policy planning staff at the State Department. A number of them—Drew Erdmann in particular—worked with me on memos, speeches, and drafts of the National Security Strategy where some of the ideas in this book were developed.

Here at the Council on Foreign Relations, where I have been since July 2003, I want to single out two individuals among many. Margaret Winterkorn-Meikle helped fulfill my many requests for articles and citations and was my all-purpose, all-star researcher. Abigail Zoba helped me juggle the responsibilities of my job with the demands of writing a book. Both Margaret and Abby were careful readers of the early, rough drafts.

A number of friends, relatives, and colleagues found or, more accurately, made the time to read drafts of what became this book and suggest changes. To Jim Hoge, Jim Lindsay, Susan Mercandetti, Jami Miscik, George Perkovich, Pete Peterson, Samantha Power, Gideon Rose, Pascaline Servan-Schreiber, Ben Sherwood, Liz Sherwood-Randall, and Benn Steil, I want to say thank you. I owe something to each and every one of you. In addition, all four of the gentlemen who were good enough to say the kind things about this book that appear on the back cover—Michael Beschloss, Bob Kagan, Henry Kissinger, and Fareed Zakaria—were also generous with their comments and insights.

I also benefited from the comments and encouragement of my agent, Esther Newberg, who defines friendship, given the fact that we are separated not just by politics but, more important, by baseball. Peter Osnos of PublicAffairs saw the possibilities in my initial proposal, and then prodded me to produce a book that could stimulate thought and debate. Clive Priddle is the sort of editor every author longs for but rarely gets: someone who challenges his thinking and adds immeasurably to the quality of his prose. Others on the PublicAffairs team—Mark Melnick (jacket design), Gene Taft (publicity), Michele Wynn (copy editor), and

Robert Kimzey (managing editor)—demonstrated equal parts talent and professionalism from start to finish.

Last, I want to thank my wife and children for putting up with me, or rather the lack of me when I disappeared to work on this book. This was not what they bargained for when I departed government, but they have been wonderful and understanding throughout.

INTEGRATION INDEX

GENERAL ORGANIZATIONS
UN Security Council

G-8

REGIONAL DIPLOMACY
Organizations

North Atlantic Treaty Org. (NATO)

Asia-Pacific Economic Cooperation (APEC)

Org. for Security and Co-operation in Europe (OSCE)

Shanghai Cooperation Org. (SCO)

Contact Groups

Six Plus Two Group on Afghanistan

Middle East Quartet

Six Party Talks on North Korea

ECONOMICS, TRADE & DEVELOPMENT
Organizations

World Bank

Paris Club

International Monetary Fund

G-7

Org. for Economic Cooperation and Dvpt. (OECD)

World Trade Org. (WTO)

China	India	Europe	Japan	Russia	USA
●		Fr, UK		●	●
		Fr, UK, Ger, It, EU	●	●	●
		Fr, UK, most EU			●
●			●	●	●
		Fr, UK, all EU		●	●
●				●	
●				●	●
		Eur. Comn.		●	●
●			●	●	●
●	●	Fr, UK, all EU, Eur. Comn.	●	●	●
		Fr, UK, most EU	●	●	●
●	●	Fr, UK, all EU	●	●	●
		Fr, UK, Ger, It	●		●
		Fr, UK, most EU	●		●
●	●	Fr, UK, all EU, Eur. Comn.	●		●

TERRORISM

Organizations

Financial Action Task Force
on Money Laundering (FATF)

UN Counter-Terrorism Committee (CTC)

Agreements

Convention on Offences and Certain
Other Acts Committed On Board Aircraft

Convention for the Suppression of
Unlawful Seizure of Aircraft

Convention for the Suppression of
Unlawful Acts Against the Safety of Civil Aviation

Convention on the Prevention and Punishment
of Crimes Against Internationally Protected Persons

International Convention
Against the Taking of Hostages

Convention on the Physical Protection
of Nuclear Material

Protocol for the Suppression of
Unlawful Acts of Violence at Airports
Serving International Civil Aviation

Convention for the Suppression of
Unlawful Acts Against the Safety
of Maritime Navigation

Protocol for the Suppression of
Unlawful Acts Against the Safety of Fixed
Platforms Located on the Continental Shelf

Convention on the Marking of
Plastic Explosives for the Purpose of Detection

International Convention for the
Suppression of Terrorist Bombing

International Convention for the
Suppression of the Financing of Terrorism

China	India	Europe	Japan	Russia	USA
		Eur. Comn.	●	●	●
●		Fr, UK, all UNSC members	●	●	●
●	●	Fr, UK, all EU	●	●	●
●	●	Fr, UK, most EU	●	●	●
●	●	Fr, UK, most EU	●	●	●
●	●	Fr, UK, most EU	●	●	●
●	●	Fr, Uk, most EU	●	●	●
●	●	Fr, UK, all EU	●	●	●
●	●	Fr, UK, most EU	●	●	●
●	●	Fr, UK, most EU	●	●	●
●	●	Fr, UK, most EU	●	●	●
		Fr, UK, most EU	●		●
●	●	Fr, UK, most EU	●	●	●
	●	Fr, UK, most EU	●	●	●

NON-PROLIFERATION & ARMS CONTROL
Organizations

International Atomic Energy Agency (IAEA)

IAEA Additional Protocol

Nuclear Suppliers Group (NSG)

Australia Group (AG)

Missile Technology Control Regime (MTCR)

Wassenaar Arrangement

Org. for the Prohibition of Chemical Weapons (OPCW)

Proliferation Security Initiative (PSI)

Agreements

Limited Test Ban Treaty

Nuclear Non-Proliferation Treaty (NPT)

Biological Weapons Convention (BWC)

Convention on Certain Conventional Weapons (CCW)

Comprehensive Nuclear Test Ban Treaty (CTBT)

Chemical Weapons Convention (CWC)

ENVIRONMENT & ENERGY
Agreements

International Energy Agency (IEA)

Montreal Protocol on Substances
that Deplete the Ozone Layer

United Nations Framework Convention
on Climate Change

Kyoto Protocol to the UNFCCC

Stockholm Convention
on Persistent Organic Pollutants

China	India	Europe	Japan	Russia	USA
●	●	Fr, UK, all EU	●	●	●
●		Fr, UK, most EU	●		
●		Fr, UK, all EU	●	●	●
		Fr, UK, all EU, Eur. Comn.	●		●
		Fr, UK, most EU	●	●	●
		Fr, UK, most EU	●	●	●
●	●	Fr, UK, most EU	●	●	●
		Fr, UK, some EU	●	●	●
	●	UK, most EU	●	●	●
●		Fr, UK, all EU	●	●	●
●	●	Fr, UK, all EU	●	●	●
●	●	Fr, UK, all EU	●	●	●
		Fr, UK, all EU	●	●	
●	●	Fr, UK, all EU	●	●	●
		Fr, UK, most EU	●		●
●	●	Fr, UK, all EU, Eur. Comn.	●	●	●
●	●	Fr, UK, all EU, Eur. Comn.	●	●	●
●	●	Fr, UK, all EU, Eur. Comn.	●	●	
●		Fr, UK, most EU	●		

HUMAN RIGHTS & CULTURAL PROTECTION

Agreements

Universal Declaration of Human Rights
Convention on the Prevention and Punishment of the Crime of Genocide
Convention to Suppress the Slave Trade and Slavery
UN Convention Against Transnational Organized Crime
Convention Against Torture and Other Cruel, Inhuman, or Degradi Treatment or Punishment
International Convention on the Elimination of All Forms of Discrimina tion Against Women

China	India	Europe	Japan	Russia	USA
●	●	Fr, UK, all EU, Eur. Comn.	●	●	●
●	●	Fr, UK, most EU		●	●
	●	Fr, UK, all EU		●	●
●		Fr, most EU, Eur. Comn.		●	
●		Fr, UK, all EU	●	●	●
●	●	Fr, UK, all EU	●	●	

NOTES

PREFACE

1. Richard N. Haass, *The Reluctant Sheriff: The United States After the Cold War* (New York: Council on Foreign Relations, 1997). Also see my "The Squandered Presidency," *Foreign Affairs*, vol. 79, no. 3 (May–June, 2000), 136–140.

CHAPTER ONE: THE OPPORTUNITY TO DEFINE AN ERA

1. See, for example, Niall Ferguson, "A World Without Power," *Foreign Policy* (July–August, 2004), 32–39, and Robert Kaplan, *The Coming Anarchy: Shattering the Dreams of the Post Cold War* (New York: Random House, 2000).
2. *The National Security Strategy of the United States of America* (Washington, DC: The White House, September 2002).
3. See *Freedom in the World 2004: The Annual Survey of Political Rights and Civil Liberties* (New York: Rowman and Littlefield/Freedom House, 2004).
4. For a recent example of such thinking, see Morton H. Halperin, Joseph T. Siegle, and Michael M. Weinstein, *The Democracy Advantage: How Democracies Promote Prosperity and Peace* (New York: Routledge/Council on Foreign Relations, 2005). For an important qualification, one that highlights how easily thin or immature democracies can be captured by nationalism, see Fareed Zakaria, *The Future of Freedom: Illiberal Democracy at Home and Abroad* (New York: W. W. Norton, 2003), 115–117.

5. See Peter G. Peterson, *Running On Empty: How the Democratic and Republican Parties Are Bankrupting Our Future and What Americans Can Do About It* (New York: Farrar, Straus and Giroux, 2004).

6. See Niall Ferguson, *Colossus: The Price of America's Empire* (New York: Penguin, 2004).

7. See Graham Allison, *Nuclear Terrorism: The Ultimate Preventable Catastrophe* (New York: Times Books, 2004).

8. See Stephen Flynn, *America the Vulnerable: How Our Government Is Failing to Protect Us from Terrorism* (New York: HarperCollins, 2004).

9. Hedley Bull, *The Anarchical Society: A Study of Order in World Politics* (New York: Columbia University Press, 1977).

10. The text of Prime Minister Blair's speech delivered at the Economic Club of Chicago on April 24, 1999, can be found at http://www.number10.gov.uk/output/Page1297.asp.

11. Henry A. Kissinger, *A World Restored: The Politics of Conservatism in a Revolutionary Age* (New York: Grosset and Dunlap, 1964), 1.

12. In addition to the work by Kissinger noted above, see two books by René Albrecht-Carrié: *The Concert of Europe* (London: Macmillan, 1968) and *A Diplomatic History of Europe Since the Congress of Vienna* (London: Methuen, 1958).

13. These should not be confused with the one attempt to make the understandings formal and explicit, the 1972 "Basic Principles" Agreement signed by the United States and the Soviet Union, which had little impact on the competition between the two superpowers, possibly because it tried to do too much.

14. See, for example, John J. Mearsheimer, *The Tragedy of Great Power Politics* (New York: W. W. Norton, 2001), Charles Kupchan, *The End of the American Era: U.S. Foreign Policy and the Geopolitics of the Twenty-First Century* (New York: Knopf, 2002), and G. John Ikenberry, ed., *America Unrivaled: The Future of the Balance of Power* (Ithaca, NY: Cornell University Press, 2002).

15. *National Security Strategy of the United States*, September 2002, 30.

16. Henry Kissinger, "A Global Order in Flux," *Washington Post*, July 9, 2004.

17. George F. Kennan, "The Sources of Soviet Conduct," in *American Diplomacy 1900–1950* (Chicago: University of Chicago Press, 1951). This is a reprint of the famous "X" article that first appeared in *Foreign Affairs* in July 1947.

18. See, for example, Norman Podhoretz, "World War IV: How It Started, What It Means, and Why We Have to Win," *Commentary* (September 2004). For more general background on the Bush foreign policy, see Ivo H. Daalder and James M. Lindsay, *America Unbound: The Bush Revolution in Foreign Policy* (Washington, DC: Brookings, 2003).

19. Sustained American unilateralism, especially if the aims were ambitious, could bring about the decline predicted by Paul Kennedy in his *The Rise and Fall of the Great Powers: Economic Change and Military Conflict* (New York: Random House, 1987).

20. See President George W. Bush's 2004 State of the Union Address of January 20, 2004. It can be found at http://www.whitehouse.gov/news/releases/2004/01/20040120-7.html.

21. For a different perspective, see Charles Krauthammer, "In Defense of Democratic Realism," *National Interest*, vol. 77 (Fall 2004), 15–25. Also see Michael McFaul, "Democracy Promotion as a World Value," *Washington Quarterly*, vol. 28, no. 1 (Winter 2004–2005), 147–163.

22. John J. Mearsheimer, *The Tragedy of Great Power Politics* (New York: W. W. Norton, 2001), 402.

23. See G. John Ikenberry, *After Victory: Institutions, Strategic Restraint, and the Rebuilding of Order After Major Wars* (Princeton, NJ: Princeton University Press, 2001).

CHAPTER TWO: A LITTLE LESS SOVEREIGNTY

1. Jessica T. Mathews, "Power Shift: The Rise of Global Civil Society," *Foreign Affairs* 76 (January–February 1997), 50–66.
2. I am indebted to both Francis Deng and Roberta Cohen, who through their work on internally displaced persons first introduced me to the seminal idea of "sovereignty as responsibility."
3. Prime Minister Blair's April 24, 1999, speech to the Economic Club of Chicago can be found at http://www.number10.gov.uk/output/Page1297.asp.
4. Sino-Russian Joint Statement, December 10, 1999. The text is at http://www.fmprc.gov.cn/eng/wjdt/2649/t15793.htm.
5. Text can be found at http://www.chinahouston.org/mews/2001615 072235.html.
6. A recent UN report articulated five criteria for the Security Council to consider before authorizing the use of force: that the threat be sufficiently serious; that the purpose is proper; that it be a last resort; that means be proportional; and that the predicted consequences of using force be more positive than those of inaction. See "Report of the High-Level Panel on Threats, Challenges and Change," *A More Secure World: Our Shared Responsibility* (New York: United Nations, 2004), 67.

CHAPTER THREE: TAKING ON TERRORISM

1. The proposed definition describes terrorism as "any action . . . that is intended to cause death or serious bodily harm to civilians or non-combatants, when the purpose of such act, by its nature or context, is to intimidate a population, or to compel a government or an international organization to do or to abstain from doing any act." (Report of the Secretary-General's High-Level Panel on Threats, Challenges and Change, *A More Secure World: Our Shared Responsibility* [New York: United Nations, 2004], 51).

2. See Richard N. Haass, ed., *Trans-Atlantic Tensions: The United States, Europe, and Problem Countries* (Washington, DC: Brookings, 1999).

3. *National Strategy for Combating Terrorism* (Washington, DC: February 2003), 12.

4. For a similar analysis, see Paul Pillar, *Terrorism and U.S. Foreign Policy* (Washington, DC: Brookings, 2001). Other thoughtful books on the subject include Daniel Benjamin and Steven Simon, *The Age of Sacred Terror: Radical Islam's War Against America* (New York: Random House, 2003); Adam Garfinkle, ed., *A Practical Guide to Winning the War on Terrorism* (Stanford, CA: Hoover Institution Press, 2004); and Audrey Kurth Cronin and James M. Ludes, eds., *Attacking Terrorism: Elements of a Grand Strategy* (Washington, DC: Georgetown University Press, 2004).

5. These comments were made on NBC's *Today Show* on August 30, 2004. See Mike Allen, "Bush Tones Down Talk of Winning Terror War," *Washington Post,* August 31, 2004.

6. Senator Kerry was quoted in Matt Bai, "Kerry's Undeclared War," *New York Times Magazine,* October 10, 2004.

7. *The 9/11 Commission Report: Final Report of the National Commission on Terrorist Attacks upon the United States* (New York: W. W. Norton, 2004), 51.

8. Anonymous (Michael Scheuer), *Imperial Hubris: Why the West Is Losing the War on Terror* (Washington, DC: Brassey's, 2004).

9. *Report of the Defense Science Board Task Force on Strategic Communication* (September 2004), 40. Available at http://www.acq.osd.mil/dsb/reports/2004–09-Strategic_Communication.pdf.

10. Natan Sharansky, *The Case for Democracy: The Power of Freedom to Overcome Tyranny and Terror* (New York: Public Affairs, 2004), 189.

11. President Bush's comments on Palestinian democracy and its relationship to peace came during his press conference with Prime Minister Tony Blair on November 12, 2004.

12. *9/11 Commission Report*, 362.

13. The most telling indictments of modern Arab societies are to be found in two works by Nadir Farjani: *The Arab Human Development Report 2002: Creating Opportunities for Future Generations* (New York: UNDP, 2002) and *The Arab Human Development Report 2003: Building a Knowledge Society* (New York: UNDP, 2003). Also see Angel M. Rabasa et al., *The Muslim World After 9/11* (Santa Monica, CA: Rand, 2004), especially chapters 1 and 2. For evidence of ferment in the Arab world, see the March 2004 Alexandria Declaration produced by a meeting of Arab intellectuals on Arab reform issues meeting at the Bibliotheca Alexandria, March 12–14, 2004, as given in *Alexandria Statement 2004: Final Statement of "Arab Reform Issues: Vision and Implementation"* 12–14 March 2004, Bibliotheca Alexandria. Available at www.pogar. org/themes/reforms/documents/alexandria.pdf.

14. See, for example, Thomas Carothers, *Critical Mission: Essays on Democracy Promotion* (Washington, DC: Carnegie Endowment for International Peace, 2004).

15. See Isobel Coleman, "The Payoff from Women's Rights," *Foreign Affairs*, vol. 83, no. 3 (May–June 2004), 80–95.

16. The Defense Science Board study on strategic communication that is mentioned above in note 9 discusses many of these issues and includes references to many other studies and reports that deal with public diplomacy. Also see Richard N. Haass, "Toward Greater Democracy in the Muslim World," a speech delivered to the Council on Foreign Relations on December 4, 2002, and published in *Washington Quarterly* (Summer 2003), 137–148; Robert Satloff, *The Battle of Ideas in the War on Terror: Essays on U.S. Public Diplomacy in the Middle East* (Washington, DC: Washington Institute for Near East Policy, 2004); and the speech by President Bush on November 6, 2003, at the twentieth anniversary of the National Endowment for Democracy (http://www.whitehouse. gov/news/releases/2003/11/print/20031106–3.html).

17. The text of the October 16, 2003, Rumsfeld memo was published in the *Los Angeles Times,* October 23, 2003.

CHAPTER FOUR: NUKES ON THE LOOSE

1. See Kenneth Waltz, *The Spread of Nuclear Weapons: More May Be Better* (London: IISS Adelphi Paper 171, 1981).
2. For background, see William J. Broad and David E. Sanger, "As Nuclear Secrets Emerge, More Are Suspected," *New York Times,* December 26, 2004.
3. Kurt M. Campbell, Robert J. Einhorn, and Mitchell B. Reiss, eds., *The Nuclear Tipping Point: Why States Reconsider Their Nuclear Choices* (Washington, DC: Brookings, 2004).
4. There is the Australia Group that seeks to limit the availability of chemical and biological materials; both the Nuclear Suppliers Group and the Zangger Committee that buttress the NPT; the Missile Technology Control Regime; and the Wassenaar Arrangement that helps to prevent the transfer of selected technologies.
5. For background, go to http://www.state.gov/t/np/rls/other/34726. htm#statement. Support is not universal. For China's objections, see Statement by the Minsitry of Foreign Affairs of the PRC, "Proliferation Security Initiative" (June 29, 2004). Text at http:// fmprc.gov.cn/eng/wjb/zjg/jks/kjlc/fkswt/t141208.htm.
6. For background, go to http://www.state.gov/t/np/rls/fs/2002/ 10316pf.htm.
7. The full text of President Bush's February 11, 2004, remarks at the National Defense University can be found at http://www.cfr. org/campaign2004/print.php?id=6762&type=pub.
8. The G-8 Action Plan on Nonproliferation (June 9, 2004) can be found at http://www.whitehouse.gov/news/releases/2004/06/ print/20040609–28.html.
9. See "Strengthening the Nuclear Non-Proliferation Regime," working paper submitted by France on May 4, 2004, to the Preparatory Committee for the 2005 Review Conference of the Parties to the Treaty on the Non-Proliferation of Nuclear Weapons (NPT/Conf.2005/PC.III/WP.22).
10. For background on the North Korean program, see *North Korea's*

Weapons Programmes: A Net Assessment (London: IISS, 2004). Also see Nicholas Eberstadt and Joseph P. Ferguson, "The North Korean Nightmare: It's Later Than You Think," *Weekly Standard* (August 30, 2004), 22–29.

11. See Joel S. Wit, Daniel B. Poneman, and Robert L. Gallucci, *Going Critical: The First North Korean Nuclear Crisis* (Washington, DC: Brookings, 2004).

12. The quotation is taken from FDR's fireside chat to the nation on September 11, 1941. The full text can be found in *The Public Papers and Addresses of Franklin D. Roosevelt, 1941* (New York: Harper and Brothers, 1950), 390.

13. See *National Security Strategy of the United States* (September 2002), 15. For some historical perspective on preventive and preemptive uses of force, see John Lewis Gaddis, *Surprise, Security, and the American Experience* (Cambridge, MA: Harvard University Press, 2004).

14. For background on the Libyan experience, see Stephen Fidler, Roula Khalaf, and Mark Huband, "Return to the Fold: How Gadaffi Was Persuaded to Give Up His Nuclear Goals," *Financial Times*, January 27, 2004. Also see Donald Mahley, "Dismantling Libyan Weapons: Lessons Learned" (paper published in November 2004 by the Chemical and Biological Arms Control Institute of Washington, DC).

15. For background on Iran's nuclear program, see Ray Takeyh, "Iran Builds the Bomb," *Survival*, vol 46, no. 4 (Winter 2004–2005), 51–63.

16. For some of the relevant recent diplomacy involving Iran's nuclear program, see Douglas Frantz, "Iran Moving Methodically Toward Nuclear Capability," *Los Angeles Times*, October 21, 2004; "Iran's Nuclear Programme, *IISS Strategic Comments*, vol. 10, no. 9 (November 2004); and Report of the Director General, "Agreement of the NPT Safeguards Agreement in the Islamic Republic of Iran," IAEA report GOV/2004/60 (September 1, 2004).

17. For the debate over the desirability and feasibility of launching a preventive strike against Iran, see James Fallows, "Will Iran Be

Next?" *Atlantic Monthly,* vol. 294, no. 5 (December 2004), 99–110; Thomas Donnelly, "A Strategy for Nuclear Iran" (AEI, October 2004); and Reuel Marc Gerecht, "The Struggle for the Middle East," *Weekly Standard* (January 3–10, 2005), 22–29. Only Gerecht comes out sympathetic to the idea.

18. Appearing on January 20, 2005, on the television show *Imus in the Morning,* the vice president said, "Well, one of the concerns people have is that Israel might do it without being asked, that if, in fact, the Israelis became convinced the Iranians had significant nuclear capability, given the fact that Iran has a stated policy that their objective is the destruction of Israel, the Israelis might well decide to act first, and let the rest of the world worry about cleaning up the diplomatic mess afterwards." The transcript is at http://www.snbc.msn.com/id/6847999.

19. For a similar approach, see "Report of an Independent Task Force," *Iran: Time for a New Approach* (New York: Council on Foreign Relations, 2004). Also see Kenneth M. Pollack, *The Persian Puzzle: The Conflict Between Iran and America* (New York: Random House, 2004), especially 375–428.

20. George F. Kennan, "The Sources of Soviet Conduct," reprinted in *American Diplomacy 1900–1950* (Chicago: University of Chicago, 1951), 104–105.

21. See, for example, Richard K. Hermann and Richard Ned Lebow, eds., *Ending the Cold War: Interpretations, Causation, and the Study of International Relations* (New York: Palgrave Macmillan, 2004).

22. See, for example, Larry Diamond, "What Went Wrong in Iraq," *Foreign Affairs,* vol. 83, no. 5 (September–October 2004), 34–56, and Thomas E. Ricks, "Army Historian Cites Lack of Postwar Plan," *Washington Post,* December 25, 2004.

23. See, for example, "Iran: A New Approach," Committee on the Present Danger (December 2004).

CHAPTER FIVE: ECONOMIC INTEGRATION

1. See, as one example, Susan Woodward, *Balkan Tragedy: Chaos and Disintegration After the Cold War* (Washington, DC: Brookings, 1995).

2. See, for example, Francis Fukuyama, *State-Building: Governance and World Order in the 21st Century* (Ithaca, NY: Cornell University Press, 2004). Also see *On the Brink: Weak States and U.S. National Security* (Washington, DC: Center for Global Development, 2004).

3. William R. Cline, *Trade Policy and Global Poverty* (Washington, DC: Center for Global Development and the Institute for International Economics, 2004), 266.

4. See Robin Wright, "Aid to Poorest Nations Trails Global Goals," *Washington Post,* January 15, 2005.

5. See Michael O'Hanlon and Carol Graham, *A Half Penny on the Federal Dollar: The Future of Development Aid* (Washington, DC: Brookings, 1997).

6. For background, go to http://www.mca.gov/about)_us/overview/index.shtml.

7. Cline, *Trade Policy and Global Poverty,* 1.

8. See Scott C. Bradford, Paul L.E. Grieco, and Gary Clyde Hufbauer, "The Payoff to America from Global Integration," in Fred Bergsten et al., *The United States and the World Economy: Foreign Economic Policy for the Next Decade* (Washington, DC: IIE, 2005), 65–109.

9. Two recent works that extol the value of trade are Jagdish Bhagwati, *In Defense of Globalization* (New York: Oxford, 2004), and Martin Wolf, *Why Globalization Works: The Case for the Global Market Economy* (New Haven, CT: Yale University Press, 2004).

10. For one comprehensive assessment of desirable trade and WTO reforms, see Peter Sutherland et al., *The Future of the WTO: Addressing Institutional Challenges in the New Millennium* (Geneva: WTO, 2004).

11. Vladimir Putin, "Address to the Federal Assembly of the Russian Federation" (May 26, 2004).

12. Edmund L. Andrews, "Rich Nations Are Criticized for Enforcing Trade Barriers," *New York Times,* September 30, 2002.

13. See Gary Clyde Hufbauer and Ben Goodrich, "Next Move in Steel: Revocation or Retaliation?" (Washington, DC: Institute for International Economics Report PB03–10, October 2003).

14. Much of the argument here is based on Jagdish Bhagwati, Arvind Panagariya, and T. N. Srinivasan, "The Muddle over Outsourcing," *Journal of Economic Perspectives,* vol. 18, no. 4 (Fall 2004), 93–114, and Daniel Drezner, "The Outsourcing Bogeyman," *Foreign Affairs,* vol. 83, no. 3 (May–June 2004), 22–34. For a view that suggests that globalization may warrant at least some reconsideration of traditional thinking as to the advantages of trade, see Paul A. Samuelson, "Where Ricardo and Mill Rebut and Confirm Arguments of Mainstream Economists Supporting Globalization," *Journal of Economic Perspectives,* vol. 18, no. 3 (Summer 2004), 135–146. Also see Aaron Bernstein, "Shaking Up Trade Theory," *BusinessWeek* (December 6, 2004), 116–120.

15. For a full discussion of this issue, see Lori G. Kletzer and Howard Rosen, "Easing the Adjustment Burden on U.S. Workers," in Bergsten, *The United States and the World Economy,* 313–341.

16. Sidney Weintraub, "Outsourcing" (Washington, DC: Center for Strategic and International Studies Issues in International Political Economy 51, March 2004).

17. For a better understanding of many of the issues involved in the debate over global climate change policy, see David G. Victor, *Climate Change: Debating America's Policy Choices* (New York: Council on Foreign Relations, 2004).

18. For a discussion of this and other aspects of the energy policy of the administration of George W. Bush, see *National Energy Policy: Report of the National Energy Policy Development Group* (Washington, DC: U.S. Government Printing Office, 2001). This group was chaired by Vice President Dick Cheney.

19. See the report of the National Commission on Energy Policy, *Ending the Energy Stalemate: A Bipartisan Strategy to Meet America's Energy Challenges* (December 2004). The text can be found at http://www.energycommission.org.

20. Amory B. Lovins et al., *Winning the Oil Endgame: Innovation for Profits, Jobs, and Security* (Snowmass, CO: Rocky Mountain Institute, 2004).

CHAPTER SIX: THE OTHER MAJOR POWERS

1. John J. Mearsheimer, *The Tragedy of Great Power Politics* (New York: W. W. Norton, 2001), 4. Also see Aaron Friedberg, "Ripe for Rivalry: Prospects for Peace in Multipolar Asia," *International Security*, vol. 18, no. 3 (Winter 1993–1994).

2. See, for example, Zhou Bian, "A Gentle Giant," *Beijing Review*, June 7, 2004, or "China's Grand Strategy," *IISS Strategic Comments*, vol. 10, no. 9 (November 2004).

3. Alexander Losyukov, "Grand Treaty, Grand Prospects," in *Mezhdunarodnaya Zhizn* (August 2001).

4. The text of Prime Minister Singh's address, delivered in New York on September 24, 2004, at the Council on Foreign Relations, can be found at http://www.cfr.org/pub7407/richard_n_haass_manmohan_singh_vishaka_desia/russell_c_leffingwell_lecture_with_manmohan_singh.php.

5. See the article by Josef Joffe, "Is There Life After Victory? What NATO Can and Cannot Do," in *National Interest*, no. 41 (Fall 1995), 19–25.

6. See "National Defense Program Guideline for FY2005 and After" and *Diplomatic Bluebook 2004: Japanese Diplomacy and Global Affairs in 2003* (Tokyo: Ministry of Foreign Affairs, 2004).

7. Henry A. Kissinger, *The Troubled Partnership: A Re-Appraisal of the Atlantic Alliance* (New York: Council on Foreign Relations, 1965).

8. The comment comes from Dominique Moisi of France. On the

state of the transatlantic alliance more broadly, see Robert Kagan, *Of Paradise and Power: America and Europe in the New World Order* (New York: Vintage Books, 2004); Philip H. Gordon and Jeremy Shapiro, *Allies at War: America, Europe, and the Crisis over Iraq* (New York: McGraw Hill, 2004); Elizabeth Pond, *Friendly Fire: The Near-Death of the Transatlantic Alliance* (Pittsburgh, PA: European Union Studies Association, 2004); Wedner Weidenfeld et al., eds., *From Alliance to Coalitions: The Future of Transatlantic Relations* (Germany: Bertelsmann, 2004); Timothy Garton Ash, *Free World: Why a Crisis of the West Reveals the Opportunity of Our Time* (London: Penguin, 2004); and Robert Cooper, *The Breaking of Nations: Order and Chaos in the Twenty-First Century* (New York: Atlantic Monthly Press, 2003), 155–172.

9. *A Secure Europe in a Better World: European Security Strategy* (Brussels: December 12, 2003), 13.

10. See China's National Defense in 2004 (China's Defense "White Paper") at http://english.people.com.cn/whitepaper/defense2004/ defense2004.html.

11. See Michael H. Armacost and Daniel I. Okimoto, eds., *The Future of America's Alliances in Northeast Asia* (Stanford, CA: Asia-Pacific Research Center, 2004), and Thomas U. Berger, *Redefining Japan and the U.S.-Japan Alliance* (New York: Japan Society, 2004).

12. David Frum and Richard Perle, *An End to Evil: How to Win the War on Terror* (New York: Random House, 2003), 247.

13. Remarks at the Institut d'Etudes Politiques, Science Politique, Paris, February 8, 2005. Text is at http://www.state.gov/secretary/ rm/2005/41973.htm.

14. *A Secure Europe in a Better World*, 12.

CHAPTER SEVEN: INTEGRATION AND THE LESSONS OF IRAQ

1. Sergei Ivanov, "As NATO Grows, So Do Russia's Worries," *New York Times,* April 7, 2004.
2. See, for example, Report of the Secretary-General's High-Level Panel, *A More Secure World,* 79–83.
3. See Gareth J. Evans and Mohamed Sahnoun, *The Responsibility to Protect: Report of the International Commission on Intervention and State Sovereignty* (Ottawa: International Development Research Centre, 2001), 55.
4. *A More Secure World,* 63.
5. See, for example, Kenneth Rogoff, "The Sisters at Sixty," *Economist* (July 24, 2004), 63–65.
6. Colin I. Bradford Jr. and Johannes F. Linn, "Global Economic Governance at a Crossroads: Replacing the G-7 with the G-20" (Washington, DC: Brookings Policy Brief 131, April 2004).
7. See Peter B. Kenen et al., *International Economic and Financial Cooperation: New Issues, New Actors, New Responses* (Geneva: International Center for Monetary and Banking Studies, 2004).
8. See "Regime Finance and Procurement" in vol. 1 of *Comprehensive Report of the Special Advisor to the DCI on Iraq's WMD* (Washington, DC: 2004). This is the so-called Duelfer report, named for Charles Duelfer.
9. On just this point, that of opportunity cost, see James Fallows, "Bush's Lost Year," *Atlantic Monthly* (October 2004), 68–84.
10. Hans J. Morgenthau, *Politics Among Nations: The Struggle for Power and Peace,* 5th ed. (New York: Knopf, 1973), 6.
11. David Frum and Richard Perle, *An End to Evil: How to Win the War on Terror* (New York: Random House, 2003), 166.
12. See Richard N. Haass, *Intervention: The Use of American Military Force in the Post–Cold War World* (Washington, DC: Brookings, 1999).

13. See, for example, Thomas P.M. Barnett, *The Pentagon's New Map: War and Peace in the Twenty-First Century* (New York: GP Putnam's Sons, 2004), 370. Barnett goes so far as to call for two armies: a "Leviathan" force for war fighting and a "system administration" force for peacekeeping-related missions.

INDEX

RICHARD N. HAASS is president of the Council on Foreign Relations. From 2001–2003 he was director of policy planning for the Department of State and both U.S. coordinator for policy toward the future of Afghanistan and the lead U.S. official for Northern Ireland's peace process. He served previously as the senior advisor on the Middle East and South Asia on the National Security Council staff of President George H.W. Bush.

PublicAffairs is a publishing house founded in 1997. It is a tribute to the standards, values, and flair of three persons who have served as mentors to countless reporters, writers, editors, and book people of all kinds, including me.

I.F. STONE, proprietor of *I. F. Stone's Weekly*, combined a commitment to the First Amendment with entrepreneurial zeal and reporting skill and became one of the great independent journalists in American history. At the age of eighty, Izzy published *The Trial of Socrates*, which was a national bestseller. He wrote the book after he taught himself ancient Greek.

BENJAMIN C. BRADLEE was for nearly thirty years the charismatic editorial leader of *The Washington Post*. It was Ben who gave the *Post* the range and courage to pursue such historic issues as Watergate. He supported his reporters with a tenacity that made them fearless and it is no accident that so many became authors of influential, best-selling books.

ROBERT L. BERNSTEIN, the chief executive of Random House for more than a quarter century, guided one of the nation's premier publishing houses. Bob was personally responsible for many books of political dissent and argument that challenged tyranny around the globe. He is also the founder and longtime chair of Human Rights Watch, one of the most respected human rights organizations in the world.

For fifty years, the banner of Public Affairs Press was carried by its owner Morris B. Schnapper, who published Gandhi, Nasser, Toynbee, Truman, and about 1,500 other authors. In 1983, Schnapper was described by *The Washington Post* as "a redoubtable gadfly." His legacy will endure in the books to come.

Peter Osnos, *Founder and Editor-at-Large*